The inauguration of Charles █ █ as president of the Universit█ █ in November of 1958 was, █ █ expressed it, "a time of rededication of the university to its function." The ten addresses delivered during the preinaugural and inaugural exercises are indicative of this rededication.

Man and Learning in Modern Society consists of these addresses, each the contribution of a distinguished scholar toward an understanding of the problems and trends of the contemporary academic world.

Three broad divisions of university discipline were examined in the preinaugural exercises: Education and Modern Society; Physical and Biological Sciences and Technology; The Humanities in the Modern World. Addresses by President Nathan M. Pusey of Harvard University, and by President Odegaard upon his inauguration, climaxed the two-day period.

Man and Learning in Modern Society makes available to scholars, students, and the public the vital observations of ten prominent men, and also provides friends and former students of the University of Washington with a permanent record of one of the university's most memorable events.

Contributors

GEORGE BOAS is professor emeritus of philosophy at Johns Hopkins University. He has California, was chancellor of the Berkeley campus before assuming his present post, and is a former associate professor in the College of Business Administration, University of Washington. Dr. Kerr is an authority on labor economics and industrial relations, and has served as a contract arbitrator for many important West Coast industries.

MAN AND LEARNING
IN MODERN SOCIETY

Man and Learning in Modern Society

PAPERS AND ADDRESSES
DELIVERED AT THE INAUGURATION
OF CHARLES E. ODEGAARD
AS PRESIDENT
OF THE UNIVERSITY OF WASHINGTON
NOVEMBER 6 AND 7, 1958

University of Washington Press
Seattle, 1959

Preface

THE PAPERS assembled in this volume were presented during the ceremonies devoted to the inauguration of Charles Edwin Odegaard as president of the University of Washington on November 6 and 7, 1958. It was the intention of those responsible for planning the program—members of the faculty, of the administrative staffs, and of the Board of Regents—to make this occasion, a significant one for the university, memorable also for the wider community.

In order to realize this goal, it was decided to invite to the campus a number of men who, by virtue of their training and achievements in a variety of fields, could be counted upon to make important contributions to an examination of the place of man and learning in modern society. Symposia were organized around three major topics: "Education and American Society," "Physical and Biological Sciences and Technology," and "The Humanities in the Modern World." Addresses by President Nathan M. Pusey of Harvard University, and by

v

President Odegaard, climaxed the two-day inaugural period.

Charles Edwin Odegaard is the twenty-fourth man to serve as the principal administrative officer of the University of Washington. He entered the office on August 1, 1958, as the successor to President Henry Schmitz, coming to Washington from the University of Michigan, where for six years he had been dean of the College of Literature, Sciences, and Arts. He received his Bachelor of Arts degree from Dartmouth College and his Master of Arts and Doctor of Philosophy degrees from Harvard University. He was a teacher of medieval history at the University of Illinois, where he was also assistant to the dean of the Graduate School, and he is a former executive director of the American Council of Learned Societies.

The inauguration brought to the University of Washington campus scores of representatives of other educational institutions and of the learned and professional societies. It was, as President Odegaard expressed it, a time of rededication of the university to its function, and the papers that follow add new depths and new dimensions to the meaning of these words. Thus the present volume is not only a record of the ceremonies connected with the inauguration, but also a record of significant approaches to education, science, and the humanities.

The university is indebted to the many persons who were helpful in the preparations for this publication. Thanks are also extended to the members of the faculty who served on the inauguration committees, presided as chairmen at the symposia, and contributed their time and inspiration to the development of a program of outstanding merit. As a result of their efforts, we shall long remember this event with gratitude and pride.

Although the primary purpose in publishing this volume is

to make available to all who may be interested the text of the addresses delivered at the inauguration, it is realized that the former students and many other friends of the University of Washington may wish to have a permanent record of the details of the inaugural events, and thus the program and accompanying notes and materials are reproduced at the end.

HAROLD S. SHEFELMAN
President, Board of Regents
University of Washington

Contents

EDUCATION AND
AMERICAN SOCIETY

CLARK KERR
President, University of California

Education for the
Scientific and Industrial Age

M R. CHAIRMAN, ladies and gentlemen—and may I add with
some justification at least—fellow Washingtonians: it is a
very great pleasure to be here to participate in this program for the inauguration of your university's president. I
am very pleased to join with you in welcoming President
Odegaard to the Pacific Coast, to extend to him the greetings of the University of California, and to express my own
personal interest in working with him for the development
of higher education in the Pacific Coast area and throughout the United States.

It is a great pleasure indeed to return here. My first regular teaching position was at the University of Washington, as
Professor Cole has just told you, and I have many friends
here. To be here brings back many warm memories. On
the way to Meany Hall, where I have attended many meet-
ings in the past, I went by my old office and inquired of
the professor who now holds it whether they had ever fixed

3

the doors on the bookcase, and he said, "No, they still stick."
But anyone coming back to the University of Washington
after an absence of several years cannot help being struck
by the tremendous growth on this campus. One sees it every
place one looks. There is, of course, even greater growth
ahead.

I am also very pleased to have the opportunity to visit the
Seattle area, where I participated at one time quite actively
in labor-relations work, and where I have many friends in
both management and the trade unions. My first arbitration
case was here in Seattle. I was then an assistant professor.
Somebody called me up one day and said he had heard
they had a professor of labor economics at the university, and
maybe I could settle a dispute they had. It was a tripartite
board, with a representative from the union, one from management, and myself as impartial member. We came out with
a unanimous decision, which proved I was "impartial," and
I was started on my career of arbitration.

I have had to curtail this career somewhat in recent years,
and particularly in recent months, and my old friends sometimes ask me how it feels not to be arbitrating any more but
to be a university administrator instead. I tell them it's all
the same thing—all mediation and arbitration. The only differences are these: I get paid a good deal less for this kind
of mediation and arbitration than for the other; and I can
no longer leave town after I have made my decisions. Beyond
that, the chief tool of the trade for a mediator and arbitrator
is unavailable to an academic administrator, and, to tell you
what that tool is, I might tell a little story. I was once back
in Washington during the war, working on an industrial
relations problem, and a friend of mine, who was also working

on an industrial relations problem, saw me from across the room. He made his way rather unsteadily across the room to me and finally got there and grasped my hand and said, "Are you working on an industrial relations problem, or are you sober?" Well, that tool of the trade, you can see, I could not use to the same extent in my present kind of mediation and arbitration.

To return to the subject of Seattle, I have been impressed by the very great growth here. As I drove past the Boeing plant last evening, I was surprised to learn that the employment of the Boeing Aircraft Company is now even higher than it was during World War II when I served as arbitrator for the Machinists' Union and for the Boeing Company and saw the great growth during that period in the Pacific Northwest. I am very pleased that Professor Ken Cole is chairman of this symposium, because I was associated with him both as a member of this faculty and as a fellow arbitrator in this area.

Now I might point out one additional thing that pleases me about these observances today and tomorrow. I have just gone through my own inauguration as the new president of the University of California. I was inaugurated on eight different campuses, and it took sixteen days to do it. It is a very pleasant contrast to see a university that can inaugurate a president in twenty-four hours.

The title for my main remarks this afternoon is "Education for the Scientific and Industrial Age," and if I had a subtitle it would be "Education for the Twenty-first Century." The University of Washington in a couple of years will be observing its hundredth anniversary, having been founded, if I remember correctly, in 1861. There have been very great changes for this university and for higher education in the United States in the century intervening since this university started with one building on a hilltop on the periphery of a wilderness, or almost a wilderness, settlement. And I would speculate that the next century will see changes as great or even greater for this university and for higher education throughout the United States.

Now whether we academicians like to admit it or not, universities throughout history have responded to their time and to their place. I do not mean to suggest that universities have no independent life of their own, because they do; nor do I mean to suggest that universities do not affect the society surrounding them. But they do respond to their time and place, and it is important to ask the question, What is the time and what is the place in relation to the university of the future? I should like to suggest, in general, that the university of the future will be more nearly a part of the vital center of society than has ever been true in the past.

We are, during this century and the century just ahead of us, undergoing the greatest change that man has ever seen on the face of this planet—a greater change than has ever occurred in the past, and perhaps greater than will ever again occur on earth. First of all, we have been going through the process of world-wide industrialization. In 1900, only one country, England, could be said to have a settled industrial way of life. Since then the United States has become industrialized, and so have Germany and Japan and, more recently and quite spectacularly, Russia. There are many other countries now in the throes of industrialization, and by the end of this century virtually the whole world will have been industrialized, resulting in the most massive transformation of the daily lives of men.

Going along with this industrialization of the world is the development of the scientific revolution that we are now experiencing. Professor Edward Teller, who is sometimes called the father of the hydrogen bomb and who is a professor of physics on the Berkeley campus, gave a speech to our students at Berkeley about a year ago in which he talked about the scientific revolution of 1650 to 2250. He made the point that in each century, beginning with 1650, man has doubled his knowledge of the physical and biological universe. Because of this doubling process, we in the 1950's are as far ahead of 1850 in our scientific knowledge as 1850 was ahead of the Age of Pericles—or even perhaps of the Stone Age. Professor Teller said that this doubling of knowledge would continue into the future and indicated some of the great discoveries that he believes will come along in the succeeding centuries as a result.

It is likely that the predictions made by Professor Teller may even be somewhat conservative. I read recently in the *New York Times* that someone had calculated that of all the trained scientists who have ever lived on earth 90 per cent are still living, and on the average they are more highly trained than the 10 per cent who have died. So we can say that we are entering what is really a new era in the history of mankind, and that this era is going to bring a greater emphasis on the worth of intellect than mankind has ever known before; and this means also a greater role for the university in society.

Now I should like to speak first of what I call the logic

of industrialization, because the industrial system does have a distinctive logic that is making itself felt throughout the world. I should like to indicate what I would call five imperatives within this logic and to point out some of their implications for education, and then turn to some of the implications for education growing out of the scientific revolution.

First of all, the industrial revolution is bringing to us a greater differentiation of tasks, a greater division of labor than even Adam Smith envisioned in his *Wealth of Nations*. More and more specialized skills at higher and higher levels are requiring university education and, beyond that, graduate education. One of the great imperatives for our universities is to turn out this vastly increasing number of more highly trained specialists. A second imperative of the industrial revolution is large-scale organizations of great complexity, and these demand continually more broadly trained executive talent. Thus we see developing in our universities this great conflict over the training of the specialist and the training of the generalist, some people saying that we should train the specialists who are the ones who make the new discoveries and the greater contribution to production, and others saying that we should be training the generalists, because if we all become specialists how can society be held together? It seems to me that this is a nonsensical debate within our universities. We cannot take the position that our major task is to train either the specialist or the generalist; rather, we must train both of them and train each of them better. The real problem, it seems to me, is how to mix the two types of training—how to relate the one to the other, so that the specialist and the generalist will not be going in opposite directions without understanding each other, unable to work well together as they must be able to do if society is to prosper.

I should like to suggest that we should be concentrating in the training of our specialists on how we can give them some general education also, particularly in the liberal arts. I am sorry to say that I think we are doing rather badly on this. At the University of California we recently made what we considered a great step forward. We instituted the requirement that our undergraduate students in engineering, who usually take four and a half or five years to earn the bachelor's degree, must take 15 per cent of their course work in fields outside engineering. Though we believe this to be a great step forward, it is probably not nearly enough in light of the fact that graduate engineers may become leaders of industry and of the country, and therefore they need to know a great deal more than engineering alone. How can we work in this general training along with the increasing demands for specialized training in the same limited time?

The parallel problem with the generalist, the person in business administration, the social sciences, or the humanities, is how to get him to understand the point of view, the approach, and the role of the specialist. I have served, as has already been mentioned, as an arbitrator, and I have seen many times the conflict in industry between the technician and the more generally trained person. We no longer have in our society to the same extent as in the past the great open battles such as those between management and labor; but increasingly the battles of today are the bureaucratic conflicts within organizations, and I sometimes think these are a great deal meaner and more destructive than the broader conflicts of decades past. And one of the great battles that goes on today is this one between the specialist and the generalist—between the time-and-motion man and the general executive, and so forth. And this would suggest that we are not doing very well at helping the specialist and the generalist to understand each other.

A third imperative of industrialization is that our society is becoming and will continue to become more and more complex all the time. This brings up the question of what then happens to the citizen. Some citizens tend to withdraw into an attitude of personal apathy, losing interest in the surrounding society, feeling that it is too big for them to understand, too large for them to affect. Or they may join some narrow special-interest group and confine their attention to this group, ceasing as a result to be general citizens. I might say that we see this happening on our campuses, and I presume that you have some of it on this campus. I know we do on the Los Angeles campus and the Berkeley campus of the University of California. You can see the students who withdraw into apathy and also the students who withdraw into narrow interest groups and cease to be responsible campus citizens. So we have the task in the university of training our students for the future, of trying to make them responsible individuals—and I would emphasize both of those words. We must try to make them feel a sense of personal responsibility and act on it as individuals.

Now a fourth imperative of this industrial society that is sweeping across the world is that it is becoming a world society. My own guess is that some day the logic of industrialization will bring about a single world culture. In some ways

I regret this, because some of the variety man has known in the past will be destroyed, as many older and weaker cultures will be supplanted; but as we move toward this world society the universities must of course respond to the new developments. I should like to mention in particular here the need to bring to the attention of our students the importance of better training in languages. It is one of the great national tragedies that, as the United States assumes more and more responsibility around the world, our diplomats, our businessmen, and our tourists visiting abroad are so little able to converse with people of other countries. I should like to suggest also that we should be paying a great deal more attention within our universities to comparative cultures and to understanding and appreciation of ways of doing things other than our own. I have served a little in foreign countries, as have some of you here this afternoon. I have found the standard American approach to be that things ought to be done exactly as we do them in the United States, in San Francisco or Seattle—with no appreciation of the different history and the different traditions that lie behind the way things are done abroad. And so the need as we assume our new position in the world to understand comparative cultures.

The fifth and final point in this logic of industrialization is that man will be enjoying more and more leisure and more and more wealth. This may result, however, in greater cultural conformity as we use our greater leisure and wealth in mass forms of consumption; but I think that one of the tasks of the university today and in the future is to teach our students to use their leisure and their wealth as independent individuals, to understand the great variety of interests in the world and the wondrous range of man's intellectual and artistic triumphs. One of the things that the "angry young men" in England are angry about is that so many people are spending the new leisure and the new wealth watching the highest-rated television program and drinking the same popular brand of beer. Is this to be the unworthy result of the new leisure and the new wealth? So we have the great task of bringing to the attention of our students while they are on the campus the exciting possibilities for the human mind, the stimulus of learning and the attitude of discovery that they can carry with them as sources of enrichment throughout their lives. This also is an imperative as we face the logic of industrialization.

May I say in summary, then, on my first two points, that we need both the specialist trained to high competence in relatively limited fields and the generalist with broad competence in many areas—each, however, having an appreciation and some comprehension of the other's work. Third, we need to impart to all our citizens an understanding of the values and requirements of all our society and of their relation to that society as individuals. Fourth, because of the increasing complexity and immediacy of our relationships with other countries, we need to achieve greater and more widespread competence in foreign languages and better appreciation of other cultures. And, additionally, our growing leisure and wealth demand an education that will help people to use these achievements at the highest possible level, thus realizing them as pure gains and not as mixed blessings.

Now at the same time that we are facing the sweep of industrialization, we have, as I mentioned before, a tremendous growth in knowledge, and I should like to mention briefly three of its impacts on the university. First of all, the great universities, including the University of Washington, are going to have to become even more devoted to research than they are today—becoming great research enterprises adding to the knowledge and wealth of our society. Second, our great universities are going to be even more involved in service to industry and agriculture and government as the new ideas discovered here are fed faster and faster into the operation of our society. Industry is no longer waiting outside the door of the laboratory for new discoveries but is almost inside the door trying to get the discoveries, sometimes before they are really made. Third, we are going to have to undertake more intensive education of all our youth, not only at the university level, but I would say particularly in the high schools of our nation. I am quite convinced that we can push back a good deal of the work that now must be given in the freshman and sophomore years of college to the high school level, thus making it possible to give expanded and enriched training in the four undergraduate years.

As a consequence of these developments, it is quite clear that we are going to have more to do in the field of education than we have ever had before—more teaching, more research, more service. And education in the United States, as you are all well aware, is now going through a great period of crisis. This, however, is not the first crisis for American education. There was one great crisis about a century ago when our universities and colleges turned away from teaching of the classics to a hereditary elite and adopted a new approach. This approach, which affected not only the universities but our whole school system, was brought about by Jeffersonian and Jacksonian democracy, which held that education should be spread more or less equally over the total population, and it was influenced also by the first impact of industrial society, which demanded so many new skills from the populace. As a result of this crisis of a century ago, we got among other things our state universities and land-grant institutions, including the University of Washington, the University of California, and many others.

This new emphasis upon equality in education and upon vocationalism came, I think, to be excessively egalitarian and excessively utilitarian. Today, as a consequence, we are facing another crisis brought about by the necessity to turn our universities, particularly our great universities, from an overemphasis on the vocational side of education and to make education more truly intellectual. This necessity grows out of the greater complexity of the modern world and the consequent need to train a new elite to run the world. The new elite will not be based on wealth and family, as in the past, but rather it will be an elite of talent. For the leading universities, which must become more intellectual and more concerned with the selection and training of this new elite, these trends have many impacts. They will affect entrance requirements, as they are doing at this university now. They will also have a great impact on the curriculum. As a result of these impacts, our leading universities will be making even greater contributions to public welfare and survival than they have made in the past. There are many implications of this, and I should like to mention one for a moment, namely, the effect in the field of athletics and athletic programs. As we face the future, the great athletic teams are going to be related, not to the size and distinction of the university, but rather to the level of the institution's entrance requirements. I think that for the great universities, including this one, there is going to be a great change in this area; and I hope that our new West Coast association to which the University of Washington belongs—the Athletic Association of Western Universities—can help chart the path to bring together those universities with the higher entrance requirements, so that better opportunity for fair competition among their student bodies may be achieved.

Now this may seem like a quite minor point in the course of my sweeping generalizations about world history and education. Having served as chancellor of the Berkeley campus of the University of California for six years, however, I have learned that athletics is not a minor matter. I commented to the academic senate one time when there was the usual parking problem up for discussion, and when I had gone through the Pacific Coast Conference controversy, and when the campus had had a panty raid that got headlines all around the world, that I had discovered that the three great academic problems—in fact I concluded the only great academic problems—were these: sex for the students, athletics for the alumni, and parking for the faculty. And I went on to say that this was a commentary not only on my job but also on the average age and consequent interests of the three groups involved.

Now, in conclusion, I have been speaking very briefly on the problems ahead as we face the impacts of industrialization and the scientific revolution on our institutions of higher education. They can be viewed as problems, but they can also be viewed as great challenges and great opportunities— and I prefer to view them that way. Great opportunities are being given particularly to the leading universities to be of more service than ever before in the history of mankind. In the course of one of George Orwell's troubled reflections on the modern world, he said: "In every country in the world, the large army of scientists and technicians, with the rest of us panting at their heels, are marching along the road of 'progress' with the blind persistence of a column of ants."

Orwell placed quotation marks around the word "progress" to emphasize his ironic intention. Do we have to accept this pessimistic description? I believe not, and I profoundly hope not. Not all change, certainly, is progress, and much of it is being forced upon us; but it is futile to lament change because we cannot arrest it. And the power our scientists and technicians are placing in our hands can be a force for genuine progress if we can produce men and women with the strength and vision to order our new knowledge and make it serve our new society.

We shall indeed need persistence in the years ahead, but assuredly it need not, and must not, be blind. The entire aim of education is precisely to prevent intellectual blindness, to dispel the darkness of ignorance and insularity and moral irresponsibility. The founders of the University of Washington chose well when they chose as their motto *"Lux sit,"* "Let there be light."

We must bend our best efforts to the tasks before us, with the confidence that we can make this scientific and industrial age an age of progress and enlightenment, not only now, but in the next century and the years beyond that.

EUGENE V. ROSTOW
Dean, School of Law
Yale University

Education for
a Society of Law

I⊤ IS A PRIVILEGE to bring to you, President Odegaard, and to
the entire University of Washington community, the greetings and congratulations of President Griswold and of the
faculty of Yale University. This is a most meaningful occasion. The investiture of a new president at any university
is more than an academic festival. It should be what this
ceremony so clearly is, a reaffirmation of, and a rededication
to, those ideals of disinterested scholarship that bind the
universities of the world into a brotherhood of transcendent
importance to the human family.

My topic this afternoon is "Education for a Society of
Law." It is a theme, as I view it, that requires me to consider the purpose of a university experience in the lives of
people viewed as members of society. I believe that the
true and final goal of our social order, and of any free
society, is to liberate the individual and to afford him every
possible opportunity for creative self-development as a

civilized person. It is the distinguishing feature of our culture that we regard this purpose as a good in itself—indeed,
as our highest good. We favor the development of people as
civilized men and women not merely because such people
are more productive workers, or better lawyers, doctors, or
politicians, but because the formation of civilized persons is
the finest achievement of a culture worthy to be called a
civilization.

One indispensable characteristic of the civilized person is
his sense of social responsibility. Because he is civilized, the
civilized man understands and accepts the burden of enlightened citizenship in a tradition that goes back beyond
Athens and has always been one of the glories of American
life. This afternoon I shall attempt to speak to that aspect
of the matter: the tithe of obligation that free men owe,
even in the most individualistic society, to the community in
which they live. Manifestly, education is one of the vital
forces that prepare men and women for the responsibilities of
freedom in a society of law, as it helps equally to prepare
them for its vistas of creativity.

I

I recently had the interesting privilege of attending a
conference of lawyers, judges, and law professors at the
Academy of Sciences of Warsaw. The theme of the conference was that moving phrase, "The Rule of Law," today
as always a central preoccupation in our life as a people.

The conference at Warsaw was the second in a series on
this topic held under the auspices of the International Asso-

ciation of Legal Science and of UNESCO. The first meeting took place at the University of Chicago in 1957. The Warsaw colloquium was directed in the first instance to the significance of the idea of the Rule of Law in the Communist states of Central and Eastern Europe. Over 120 lawyers from more than 20 countries assembled in the beautiful and contradictory capital of Poland for 8 days of professional discussion and debate.

Warsaw was a suggestive setting for these talks. The rebuilding of Warsaw and the other war-ravaged towns of Poland is one of the extraordinary, and least-known, events of the postwar world. Poland is at best a poor country, and it was drained white by the war. Until 1956 it functioned under increasingly effective Communist control. Today the Poles fear an approaching end for the period of autonomy that followed their successful defiance of the Russians in 1956. The signs are multiplying that in Poland, as in more tractable parts of the Soviet Empire, the thaw is being succeeded by a new freeze, although thus far the freeze is not so bitter as that of Stalin's era.

Despite these forbidding circumstances, however, the plan of reconstruction in Poland goes forward. It bespeaks an altogether different influence. The plan of reconstruction was adopted before the complete taking over of control in Poland by the Communists. Under it, the Poles have rebuilt their historical churches, palaces, squares, and old buildings, down to the medieval walls and moats. With brilliant taste, and a fierce and united devotion to the task, they have erected a monument to the power of the ideas that matter in the life of a people. Mile after mile, in large towns and in small ones, the traveler sees baroque market places and court-

yards, merchants' houses of the seventeenth and eighteenth
centuries, long, curving streets, restored so perfectly that it is
impossible to believe they are not what they seem to be.
Statues, plaques, and gardens memorialize the kings and
heroes of Poland, Chopin and Copernicus, Sigismund and
Joseph Conrad, names that vibrate in the memory of the
Polish people. Receptions are given in spacious eighteenth-
century rooms with parquet floors, green marble columns,
mahogany tables, Louis Seize chairs. There are, of course,
modern roads, great blocks of apartment houses, and other
familiar contemporary landmarks. But a large part of the daily
life of each city, and of many villages, takes place in its old
buildings.

Was this gigantic and most expensive effort a romantic
folly? It more than doubled the cost of reconstruction in
Poland and delayed the rehousing of the people by several
years at least. Yet I met no Pole who thought the policy
wrong, despite the discomforts of the housing problem. And
I was assured on high authority that there is, and indeed
could be, no Polish criticism of the decision. All Poles are
proud of this tremendous national achievement, which has
restored to the people the visual image of their country's
identity and of its past. The political and cultural meaning
of the program is apparent. Its consequences will no doubt
be felt for centuries to come.

The city of Warsaw was thus a most appropriate back-
ground for a conference devoted to the role of ideas in
human affairs. For it would be hard to imagine more dramatic
evidence to deny the Marxian thesis that economic and material factors are paramount in the social process.

The conference itself dealt with this theme as directly as

the conventions of public discourse between East and West now permit. The speakers from the Communist countries all started by distinguishing the idea of the Rule of Law to which they aspired—the concept of Socialist legality, as they called it—from mere order. In any organized community, however tyrannical, they pointed out, there is general obedience to law and acceptance of its authority. There is more to the Rule of Law, they said, than acquiescence in the commands of the state. They were clearly in the camp of Locke and Montesquieu, not of Hobbes. To qualify as the Rule of Law, a legal system must meet certain standards identified as those of humanism. It must provide legal protection for the civil rights of individuals. There should be regular procedures for consulting citizens about policy. In these libertarian times, legal authority can be legitimately derived only from the people's consenting will. The state should be subject to the law, and there should be higher institutions of the law, staffed by independent judges, to correct errors, coordinate the decisions of lower courts, administrators, and administrative bodies, and in this way help to assure all citizens equal treatment before the law.

At the level of abstraction, the Western lawyers could hardly quarrel with this approach to the task of defining the elements of a civilized legal system. We asked many questions, of course, about the relation of these norms to practice in the Communist countries. But our questions, and the answers to them, were not the most interesting part of the conference. To me, at least, the striking and important aspect of the discussion was the significance of the definition of the Rule of Law that the Eastern speakers had offered.

For in its tenor the concept of legality they proposed

represents the weight and power of the entire Western tradition of law. Its values are distilled from thousands of years of thought and experience, extending to the Roman law and to more ancient influences. It has grown, theme by theme, in considered adaptation to many cycles of social and political change. The law is part of its social matrix, at any moment of history, but it is also an independent and autonomous social force, a cause as well as a consequence. Influenced by events, it influences them in turn, in the name of abiding human purposes that give it life.

What struck me sharply at Warsaw is that there is only one Western tradition of law, and that Marxism has not produced an alternative to it. Marx, after all, wrote little about law, and then not helpfully. Marx came to the study of economics from his study of law, and particularly of Hegel's philosophy of law. He was led by his studies, he wrote, to the conclusion that legal relations as well as forms of state could neither be understood by themselves nor be explained by the so-called general progress of the human mind. They are rooted, he concluded, in the material conditions of life. "The mode of production in material life," he wrote, "determines the general character of the social, political and spiritual processes of life." [1]

This thought he later summed up in the proposition that political power and law were merely the organized power of one class for oppressing another—or, in the phrase of one of his followers, "the union of the master class formed to safeguard exploitation." In Marx's view, the law of nine-

[1] Karl Marx, *A Contribution to the Critique of Political Economy* (1859), translated from the second German edition by N. I. Stone (Chicago: Charles H. Kerr and Co., 1911), p. 11.

teenth-century Europe and the United States was a system devised to accomplish the exploitation of the working classes by the bourgeoisie.

The speakers of Warsaw did not give more than lip service to such passages from Marx or his followers, and in many cases there was not even lip service. These men were trained as lawyers in the common literature of Continental law. And their minds were irrevocably shaped by that massive and intricately woven structure. They were products —prisoners, if you like—of their legal education. They took as natural premises the familiar axioms I have just restated, without pretending to explain where they came from, beyond vague references to "humanism" or, in a more orthodox vein, to "Socialist humanism." The Declaration of the Rights of Man was quoted more often than any document of the Russian Revolution or the Socialist hagiography. And a Polish speaker summed up the concept of the Rule of Law in Lincoln's phrase, "Government of the people, by the people, and for the people."

The papers delivered at the conference were not all great works of philosophy or juristic science. Nor is it very important that some probably had a considerable content of cynicism or hypocrisy. After all, hypocrisy is the classic tribute of vice to virtue. It is no small victory for the ideas of our civilization if its enemies are forced to profess their faith in them. Once upon a time, tyranny did not need to apologize. The sword, in those days, was its own guarantee of legitimacy.

What is worth remarking, I think, is the testimony of these Communist students of law to the ultimate power of ideas in the process of social change. I rather teased them with being idealists, rather than materialists. For they clearly demonstrated the way in which certain accepted norms of behavior, not peculiar to any particular social system, provided them with their only criteria of judgment and thus helped to fix the course of their proposals for legal development within their own communities. In that way, the abiding tradition of Western law is exerting a creative influence on the evolution of legal institutions in Communist Europe. The civilized values of the lawyers have not, of course, fully prevailed in central and eastern Europe. In my judgment, they cannot prevail so long as the dictatorship of the Communist Party denies any meaning to the concept of popular sovereignty and to the independence of the judges. If, as these lawyers know better than we, they cannot win entirely, it is clear that they are working hard for half a loaf. Along with many writers, poets, and ordinary men, they represent in the Communist societies a steady assertion of purposes that must constantly be at war with those of tyranny. The lawyers and high officials are divided within themselves. They know they are captives, willing or unwilling as the case may be, of regimes that could not survive a free election. But one persistent part of their minds cannot accept the situation in which they find themselves. The struggle goes on, within their souls and between them and the Party.

II

It is no paradox for Americans to acknowledge the force of ideas and of ideals in human behavior. And it is a cliché for our people to assert their belief in the Rule of Law, in this sense, as the organizing principle of our society and of other Western democracies. No sonorous speech to a bar association, no flight of fancy at a commencement, is complete without such an invocation. But does this thesis, all too glibly accepted, really correspond to the present truth about our social condition?

The Western legal tradition, in its special American form, has had an excellent opportunity to flower in our country. And it has enjoyed, and enjoys today, a turbulent vitality appropriate to its role. In an open society, where the law must mediate conflicts of all kinds, the law is an indistinguishable part of the life of action. It cannot be altogether above the fray.

Within recent years, however, strong voices have attacked not particular rules of law but the Rule of Law itself. We have heard bitter attacks by nihilists and know-nothings on our basic legal procedures for safeguarding the individual against the threatening power of the state. The Chief Justice remarked a few years ago that he wondered whether the Bill of Rights could muster up a popular majority if it were put to a vote today. I believe the Constitution and its Bill of Rights would prevail in an election today, as they did in the closing years of the eighteenth century. But there have been moments recently when no one could deny the pertinence of the Chief Justice's question.

For some time now a smoldering revolt against the Rule of Law has been developing in our culture. The revolt stems primarily from the dilemma of our brothers in the South, required, in the name of the law, to accelerate the pace of social change in their communities. It draws strength, too, from the comparable feelings developed in many Northern cities, which must adjust to the same difficult processes of racial accommodation.

There is clearly something beginning to approach organized underground movements at work in the United States. Coercion, intimidation, boycott, and worse are common occurrences in many parts of the country. Since January, 1957, there have been sixty-seven bombings or attempted bombings in the South alone. Not a single person has yet received a jail sentence for these outrages. Comparable episodes have occurred in Pennsylvania, Illinois, and other places in the North.

We must seek to mobilize the decent, law-abiding opinion of the country to deal constructively with this problem throughout the nation. Indeed, we are long overdue in undertaking such action. A great educational effort should be made, under the leadership of the President, to help restore a climate of respect for law. Within that climate, the President, the Congress, and the governments of the several states could and should, together and in agreement, hammer out workable approaches to progress in race relations throughout the nation, in Chicago as well as in Little Rock, in New York as well as in Norfolk. These approaches should be primarily local, educational, and voluntary, although some further national and state legislation and administrative action may be needed to give the movement momentum and direction. Governor Collins of Florida has twice recently called for such action. His wise and urgent call should be heeded.

Like all revolutionary acts, this incipient rebellion appeals to deep and intangible loyalties that compete in the minds of men with their loyalty to the Rule of Law itself. It has drawn many well-meaning people most unwillingly into the camp of resistance to the law. The cleavage widens as we watch the appalling spectacle of governors and legislatures openly seeking to evade and defy the law they have sworn to uphold. Many who should be working with the President and the Congress to devise sound procedures for complying with the law have chosen, for the moment at least, to devote their energies to programs of nullification. Meanwhile the majority opinion, loyal to the law, works silently but may well be losing ground to the extremists.

These somber and disquieting events cast a shadow over the whole nation.

The values of our constitutional tradition will prevail in this struggle, I firmly believe, as they have prevailed in all the previous struggles of our public life. They will prevail because they pervade and dominate our culture and the operative value systems of the large majority of our people. But they will not prevail without active and courageous leadership to deal with our present troubles about race relations. And in the long run they will not prevail unless our people are taught to know them, to understand them, and to accept them as the very bones of their being.

Many have wondered whether our civilization is failing to perpetuate itself. Gloomy observers shake their heads over the present state of our family life. They note the apparent rise of juvenile delinquency and other signs that seem to indicate an alienation of considerable numbers of young people from the main stream of the culture. They call attention to widespread political apathy, in an environment that seems to lack dramatic political issues, although that fact, bespeaking the general unity of our people, is hardly in itself a condition to deplore. They comment on the weight of powerful organizations in our society—corporations, trade unions, the armed forces, government itself—huge masses of hierarchy that seem to threaten the possibility of meaningful personal freedom for the individual. And they turn to our systems of education, sprawling and diverse, and ask whether they are the source of all our troubles.

Let me say at once that I do not share the forebodings of the prophets of gloom. It has always been difficult to transmit the values of the past to the independent and rebellious minds of the young, and it is especially difficult to do so in a society of free men that notoriously has no particular reverence for age, dignity, and the pomp of high place.

III

Even if the Jeremiahs are wrong, however, we should hardly rely on automatic forces, or the weight of the past, to preserve values of such basic importance to the future of society. How can we assure ourselves that we are doing our best to educate men and women for a society of law? From what sources can we teach the population at large respect for the procedures, institutions, and values of law as they have developed in our constitutional universe?

I suggest that three phases of our life have roles of special responsibility in this educational process: first, legal education, both in professional schools of law and in the liberal arts curriculum; second, the quality of the legal system, in its day-to-day functioning; and, finally, the state of our educational system and our cultural life generally.

As water cannot rise above its source, so law, for all its continuity, cannot do much more than express and articulate the values of the culture at large. The law of a society cannot be much richer or more humane than its art or its literature; like them, it represents the values by which its people live.

Ezra Stiles, an early president of Yale, thought that the study of law at universities could do much to this end. In 1777, he urged the teaching of law not only to improve the professional training of lawyers, but to help form citizens as "civilians. . . . It is scarcely possible," he said, "to enslave a Republic where the Body of the People are Civilians, well instructed in their Laws, Rights and Liberties." The training of university students in law, President Stiles urged, would be "catching; it propagates to all around and transfuses itself thro' the public. . . . How Happy a Community abounding with men well instructed in the Knowledge of their Rights and Liberties." There is no doubt a great deal to be said for the diffusion of understanding about law through the influence of university law schools and through the study of law in nonprofessional terms as part of the liberal arts curriculum at the college level. Such currents of thought can surely do good in translating the values of the tradition of humanism into legal forms and in overcoming the general ignorance of the nonprofessional population about the purposes and methods of law. I used to ask dinner guests who belonged to rarefied circles in other departments of the Yale faculty what the writ of habeas corpus was. I was astonished to discover an almost universal absence of knowledge about that most fundamental weapon in the armory of our freedom.

How should we define the duty of the university law

schools, and of the study and teaching of law at the universities, in this perspective? As I have said elsewhere:

> Legal scholarship, like other branches of scholarship, can justify itself only if it maturely faces the big issues in our path—the fundamental, perennial legal issues of liberty, order, and social justice, which appear before us in a contemporary garb.
>
> The thought behind this pursuit is not merely the ancient loyalty of all university men to the faith in knowledge as a good to be sought for its own sake. We are indeed communicants in that profession. But the study of law, and the practice of law, are meaningful only as parts of the quest for justice. The pursuit of law is not sufficiently explained as a phase of the search for knowledge. It is that, of course. But it is more, too. No act of law is valid without moral sanction. The animating premise of law practice, of the judges' work, and of legal scholarship is that law should improve the means through which society seeks to carry out the promises of its code.
>
> We are at a period in our history as a nation when we are peculiarly dependent on our own intellectual resources for the kind of original thought which can illuminate opinion, and prepare the way for wise resolutions in the growth of law. If the purposes of American law are to be fulfilled, we shall need, as never before, bold and inventive ideas drawn from our intellectual life—ideas good enough to earn a place in the realm of the spirit.[2]

As we view the state of the legal order in the United States, demanding tasks loom up. If the legal system is to remain healthy and successful, these tasks will have to be discharged. There are acute social conflicts to be resolved in the spirit of the legal tradition, adjustments to be made in adapting our society to the changing contours of world politics. We face a long catalogue of issues, large and small, which require legal action based on careful study and understanding

[2] "Report of the Dean of the Yale Law School for the Years 1954-1956, December 15, 1956," *Bulletin of Yale University*, Series 52, No. 24, p. 6.

before we can expect tensions to be diminished and social progress to continue.

> The law schools should not be dominated by the issues which happen to be topical or dramatic at any given moment. The universities are universities, after all, not departments of government. And the immediate, politically exciting issues are often superficial or transient reflections of more fundamental legal or social problems. Giving due weight to this truism, the university law schools should, however, be continuously interested in the underlying policy problems of contemporary law.[3]

The goal of all such efforts is the improvement of the legal order. Two phases of this task should be distinguished. The first is the endless struggle of each society more fully to realize its own ideal of law—to bring the law in action more nearly into harmony with the law on the books. The second, and perhaps the more important, is the role of the law as one among many forces seeking further improvement in the society's ideal of law.

While I believe in the social utility of studying law at our universities—indeed I have a vested interest in that conviction—there is a more powerful influence at work. The most important force teaching people to understand the real nature of law is that of experience and example. We cannot expect to persuade men that the law is fair and decent if they know it to be cruel and corrupt. They will not believe in due process of law if at the station house policemen give prisoners the third degree. They will turn away in cynical despair when men proclaim equality before the law if the manifest truth is that it continues to condone inequality.

The tradition of law is an autonomous force exerting great and pervasive influence in the life of society. As we can see

[3] *Ibid.*, p. 7.

in Poland and the Soviet Union, it can survive for a time, perhaps for a long time, even in a hostile environment, and be not without some consequence in that environment. But the law, after all, is simply the expression in institutional form of certain agreed upon values. Those values develop and find other outlets in the whole body of a culture. They embody views as to the dignity and importance of each individual which emerge from the moral history of the human race. Concepts of justice and order develop as social life takes on new forms and reaches new stages. They have a tenacious continuity, too, based on past experience as interpreted for us by the most gifted artists, philosophers, jurists, and writers of our cultural history.

But the goals of the legal order are those of the culture at large. Judge Learned Hand, one of the greatest of our judges, said a few years ago that no court can save a society so riven that it has lost the spirit of moderation, its almost instinctive adherence to the fundamental principles of equity and fair play that our constitutions enshrine.

> What is the spirit of moderation? It is the temper which does not press a partisan advantage to its bitter end, which can understand and will respect the other side, which feels a unity between all citizens—which recognizes their common fate and their common aspirations—in a word, which has faith in the sacredness of the individual. If you ask me how such a temper and such a faith are bred and fostered, I cannot answer. They are the last flowers of civilization, delicate and easily overrun by the weeds of our sinful human nature; we may even now be witnessing their uprooting and disappearance until in the progress of the ages their seeds can once more find some friendly soil. But I am satisfied that they must have the vigor within themselves to withstand the winds and weather of an indifferent and ruthless world; and that it is idle to seek shelter for them in a courtroom. Men must take that temper and that faith

with them into the field, into the marketplace, into the factory, into the council-room, into their homes; they cannot be imposed; they must be lived. Words will not express them; arguments will not clarify them; decisions will not maintain them. They are the fruit of the wisdom that comes of trial and a pure heart; no one can possess them who has not stood in awe before the spectacle of this mysterious Universe; no one can possess them whom that spectacle has not purged through pity and through fear—pity for the pride and folly which inexorably enmesh men in toils of their own contriving; fear, because that same pride and that same folly lie deep in the recesses of his own soul.[4]

The law is an immense social and educational influence, which can do much to assure the realization of its values in the life of society. I fully agree with Judge Hand, however, that the law cannot assure these ends single-handed. It is among the strong pillars of civilization. But it is not omnipotent in a society of democratic freedom. The values of the Rule of Law cannot prevail forever in a society that has turned away from its premises.

The universities are important among those charged with responsibility as guardians of the faith, although their responsibility is by no means exclusive. I should define their function in this respect in these terms: the universities will serve to advance the tradition of humanism, and the concept of the Rule of Law that is an indistinguishable part of it, by developing first and foremost as centers of mature and creative scholarship. Universities are bands of scholars devoted primarily to the lonely search for the advancement of knowledge. The scholar's quest for truth, like the struggle of other artists, has meaning only as an expression of the un-

---

[4] "The Contribution of an Independent Judiciary to Civilization" (1942), in *The Spirit of Liberty: Papers and Addresses of Learned Hand* (2nd ed.; New York: Alfred A. Knopf, 1953), pp. 164-65.

touchable dignity, power, and integrity of the free person.
The effort of the scholar to state his own view of the universe
is a matter of supreme importance in itself to a society that
believes in stopping its intervention at the threshold of a
man's house, and of his soul.

The teaching and training of students that has always
occurred at universities is vital and effective insofar as it is
drawn from the true scholarly work of the teachers. Not all
scholars can meet university standards of teaching. But I am
deeply persuaded that no one can teach well, and with abiding force, unless he is a scholar first. The study of the
humanities and sciences at this level in the universities of the
country is an indispensable part of the embracing process by
which we should seek to preserve and to improve the quality
of our culture, viewed as a civilization.

IV

If the institutions of the law—the courts and the legislatures, the bar associations and the law schools—approach their
duties in this spirit; if the universities continue to develop
as scholarly centers, advancing the values of the tradition
of humanism, I have no fears for the future of law in the
United States. The people will absorb a large part of the
spirit of our laws through the best of all learning processes,
direct experience. And they will come more and more completely to understand the goals and values of the law as an
integral part of their educational formation.

I believe, as I am sure you do, that in their great majorities
the American people want to progress within the framework of their constitutional past, and recoil from the very

thought of abandoning it. Our people do not yearn for tyrants or the rules of a police state. They are loyal to the ideas of the Constitution and its Bill of Rights and eager to have our society fulfill their stirring aspirations more and more completely. So long as our universities train leaders incapable of betraying these ideals, so long as the law schools and the legal profession press forward to advance this vision of the Rule of Law, we shall preserve, and indeed improve, our Society of Law—a civilization ordered not by force alone, but by its dream of justice.

Boris Pasternak poses the endless battle between Leviathan and the Rule of Law in a striking passage:

> I think that if the beast who sleeps in man could be held down by threats—any kind of threat, whether of jail or of retribution after death—then the highest emblem of humanity would be the lion tamer in the circus with his whip, not the prophet who sacrificed himself. But don't you see, this is just the point —what has for centuries raised man above the beast is not the cudgel, but an inward music: the irresistible power of unarmed truth, the powerful attraction of its example.[5]

[5] *Doctor Zhivago* (New York: Pantheon, 1958), p. 42.

ERWIN D. CANHAM
Editor, Christian Science Monitor

Education and the
Problem of Communication

WHAT IS THE problem of communication?
It is to make sure that we understand one another.

And, in these latter days, it is quite clear that a great number of us do not understand one another. It is equally clear that, if we do not make more progress in mutual comprehension, civilization and all the values of our lives are in very great jeopardy. So the problem of communication is simply one more paraphrase for the great question of our day: can we live in peace?

We are in an age when the technical possibilities of communication are utterly miraculous. It is now entirely feasible for one person's words to be heard by every other person in the world at once. You can eavesdrop on a global scale.

If anybody had told our grandfathers that the day would come when communication could be instantaneous and total, they might well have thought the millennium was at hand. They might have averred that misunderstanding would be impossible at a time when everybody could hear anybody else. The wonders of communication (like those of transportation) might have seemed certain to usher in the golden age.

It has turned out differently. We know now that the technical marvels of communication have, if anything, made misunderstanding more acute. We now know that what we say is vastly more important than the speed or ubiquity with which we say it. And so the problem of communication becomes one of content. What is it we must say? What is it to which we must listen?

(I interject at once the idea of listening because its importance is often obscured. Nowadays everybody seems to be talking at once. We have a Voice of America, but the only Ear of America we have is related to espionage. And yet it is more blessed to listen than to talk. God gave us two ears but only one voice. Especially in our international relations, we need to listen much more than we need to talk. This is elementary. What good salesman does not know it? Or what wise wife?)

What, then, is it that we must say? What is it to which we must listen? What does education have to do with it? Everything, of course. For education is the mold of society. Wherein has it failed us in our search for understanding of one another? I hold that there is nothing wrong with educa-tion, or right with it for that matter, which is not also wrong or right with the totality of American society. And the same thing applies to other systems, including the Soviet.

So let us come to the heart of the matter.

For the last decade or more, it is quite evident that the United States has failed to communicate adequately or ac-

curately to most people in other parts of the world a true
picture of its own society. The failure is doubtless due to
our own misunderstanding of ourselves. It is equally true, it
seems to me, that we have not got our values quite straight
and have altogether misconceived the significance of our material successes.

One of the great problems of this era is to understand the
meaning of man's new relationship to nature. The big
change in our times is this new relationship. In almost every
respect, men have learned new ways to control and utilize
their material environment. Incalculably vast power resources
have been organized. It is a long stride from the hoe and the
bullock to the atomic reactor—or the hydroelectric power
dam, for that matter—but we have come all this way in a
few decades, and in some parts of the world the transition
is taking place almost overnight.

In the field of transportation we have made the world a
shrinking sphere. A few weeks ago, as I was flying in
Boeing's new 707 jet from Iceland to Labrador, the sun
stood still for us. When the plane took off at Keflavik, Iceland, the sun was low in the western sky. It stood still and
then rose a little as we flew directly westward at those
northerly latitudes. This experience is already almost a commonplace for the pioneers of air travel, and soon it will be
outmoded by many other tricks of time and space.

Already, many are discussing the baffling question of what
happens to man—biologically as well as timewise—when his
vehicles fly at speeds approaching the speed of light, and
his traditional earthbound methods of calculating time become inoperable. Will space travel by-pass biology? Such
questions are still some distance in the future. Yet today and

tomorrow, literally, we have the explicit possibility of cross-
ing time zones at such speed that men's sleep habits and
their stomachs have not caught up with the society in which
they move. Thus—and in many more urgent degrees—
does transportation alter our age-old relationship to our
physical environment.

And I have already spoken of the way in which communication miracles make it possible for one person to speak
to anybody or everybody else in the world at once. Thus,
in countless significant respects, men have achieved a vast
dominion over the world in which they live. This accom-
plishment, which ought to have strengthened their awareness of the spiritual factors that have made the triumph
possible, has in fact seemed to increase their materialism. It
has stimulated a false sense of values—or the apparent acceptance of a false sense of values—in much of the Western
world.

We have placed the accumulation of material goods and
the gratification of human wants very high in our scale of
values. Conspicuous consumption has become a way of life.
We have neglected many elements of the true welfare while
we accepted the goals of the welfare state. We have devoted
too much attention to appearance and too little to reality—
too much to the physical elements of our lives and too little
to their content.

The problem is very visible in education. Some of the
finest teaching is done in some of the oldest and dingiest
buildings; some of the most banal and meretricious aspects
of the educational process take place in the most glittering
of modern surroundings. In the words of August Heckscher,
"in trying to create highways that would be perfectly safe,

we have succeeded in putting the driver to sleep, thus raising new dangers more deadly than the turns and crossroads, the hills and passing villages, which we eliminated at so great a cost."

This is not to say that superhighways should not be built —or new school buildings, either—but that we must find ways to stay awake on the highways and seek and communicate the best truth we know in the classrooms. It is not impossible to stay awake on the superhighways of modern life, it is only more difficult to do so. It is not impossible to do stern creative work in a beautiful and seductive climate, it is only more difficult to do so. Whether it is harder to teach a tough curriculum in an ultramodern schoolroom, I would not know. I suspect that, in broad terms, it is no easier. Speaking as one who is very easily distracted, I find it difficult not to gaze dreamily out of picture windows. But, then, I used to gaze dreamily at the blank wall in the one-room schoolhouse in Maine where I began my schooling, so perhaps I have little or no point here.

But, in terms of our national society itself, we certainly need to be reminded of the grim urgency of the challenge we face. It is survival. I am not privy to any special governmental or defense secrets, but I can read and listen. And it is quite apparent that the assumptions that global war would be prevented because it is too horrible, or because there will be inevitable retaliation upon an aggressor power, are no longer valid. It may or may not be possible for an aggressor power to calculate on striking a crushing blow without retaliation. The experts differ, but many of them think the calculation of victory without significant retaliation could definitely be made at a not distant date by the men in the

Kremlin. There is also the chance of miscalculation, which may be the gravest danger of all. And there is the possibility of irresponsibility or madness.

Thus the physical peril of the society in which we live is potentially grave. But the fact that affairs have reached this pitch, or something like this pitch, is the gravest fact of all. Where did we fail? What should we do now?

We failed, it seems to me, in a number of respects. In simplest terms, we underestimated the capabilities—in science, technology, and morale—of the Soviet Union. We seem not to have kept up in the armaments race. But a far graver failure was our inability to find the terms of accommodation and of peaceful change in our relations with the Soviet Union. Deeper still was our failure to stiffen the will and strengthen the values of our own people.

In the words of Senator Fulbright, these years of the 1950's have been marked for us by a weakness for the easy way. The easy way, diplomatically and militarily, was to wage the cold war—but, alas, to do it ineffectively. It is bad to wage war at all, but the worst crime is to wage war ineffectively. Far better, of course, would have been to make peace. We have said repeatedly that we were seeking "situations of strength" from which we could make peace. Unhappily, we seem to have failed to achieve or to retain the situations of strength. Within the terms of our effort to wage the cold war, to achieve containment of the Communist states, to cope diplomatically with many acute crises, it can be said that American policy has achieved certain local successes. It has prevented—or helped to prevent—or at least not stimulated the outbreak of any great war; it has curbed the spread of Communist power into many areas. In its day-to-day fashion it has often been tireless and sometimes ingenious. But always the United States has been one jump behind: responding to situations, instead of creating them; fighting rear-guard actions; running terribly hard in the effort to stay in the same place.

Thus we must revise our basic premises. But more important than our military decline, surely, is our decline in morale and determination, our misplacement of values. In a period of change, we did not re-examine and revise the effectiveness and validity of our institutions and our methods of operating them. But now the question is: what do we do now?

Until firm and enforceable agreements to limit and control armaments have been reached, we have no other alternative than to try to bring our defenses up to a deterrent level and keep them there. In that task, however, we should understand that the physical forces solve no problems and are merely a concession to our failure to achieve a deeper security. Our safety lies not in the devising and piling up of ever more fiendish and efficient methods of destruction. These can never really save man.

Our real problem, of course, is to set in motion the conditions that will make possible effective reduction and control of armaments. We cannot destroy Communist power in the world by military force. It is both impossible and unthinkable. But we can contribute to conditions that will make it possible to live with an evolving Russian state and Chinese state. One point upon which returning travelers from the Soviet Union are in deep and emphatic agreement is the intense desire of the Soviet peoples for peace, whatever may be the position of their government. This is a force not to be ignored. What the state of mind of the Chinese peoples may be is more obscure; we have chosen to cut ourselves off from adequate sources of information on the subject.

Earlier I mentioned the importance of listening, as well as talking. One of the most valuable exercises we could attempt would be to try to understand how our actions appear to other people—and above all to the Soviet people. We are more or less confident of the purity of our intentions, of the strictly defensive nature of our military posture. But what we have done must look far different to the Soviet people and to their leaders. Our outposts from Quemoy to Turkey fringe the very harbors and frontiers of the Communist world.

Spurred by our activities, they seem now to have placed themselves very close to a position of military superiority. Scarcely ever have we mounted a serious attempt to persuade the Russians that we are not seeking to overthrow their form of government and perhaps dominate their state. We have repeatedly and overtly declared our intention to help in destroying the satellite governments that are the Soviet Union's ring of buffer states—their Canadas and Mexicos.

From our viewpoint, and the true one, our determination is to help the peoples of these tragic nations to regain their own freedom and right of choice. Sometimes we encourage them to expect more help than they will receive. The slogan of "liberation" was tragic because it was ineffective. Its only real meanings were a false encouragement to the satellite peoples and a direct and flagrant challenge to the Kremlin. Thus, as seen from Moscow, our global position is a serious threat to the security of the Soviet Union.

Scarcely any of our actions can look peaceful as viewed from the other side. Inept they may sometimes appear, but scarcely ever very friendly. I do not wish to be naïve or gullible, or to overestimate this factor, but in my personal experience and observation nearly always when an American has done something that was generous and kind toward a Soviet person, and was so understood, he has met with a warm and exuberant response. In grim realism, I know that much of our relations must be conducted in very hard-boiled terms; that military elements are eloquent; that Communist ideology is hard and treacherous and blinds the individual to reality and truth. But, all the same, I believe it will always be valuable to understand just how we look to the other side, and to try friendliness and kindness whenever we can.

Our hope and goal, of course, is for the evolution of communism in the Soviet Union and China until it no longer seeks to destroy by military force the freedoms of other nations and societies. It is not clear that communism alone is the source of this imperialism. Manifestly, if China and the Russian states were organized under some form of Fascistic or Nazi totalitarianism, their military threat would be no less, except to the important degree that the present threat is aided by subversion. Furthermore, other degrees of nationalism—including old-fashioned monarchy or imperialism —might be almost as expansionist. Just what the world relations of Russia or China would be if their form of government were that of a representative republic or democracy— and if this government had the elements of industrial and social strength of the United States or western Europe or of the British Commonwealth—is an interesting speculation. The exuberance, dynamism, and inherent power of the

Russian and the Chinese peoples would be forces to reckon with in the world in any case.

And, even if the aggressive tendencies of these two great powers were to vanish in our world overnight, the United States would still face grave world-wide problems and challenges. The surge of the awakening peoples of Asia and Africa—what Lothrop Stoddard long ago called "the rising tide of color"—is an underlying aspect of the problem. At any rate, the explosive force of awakening peoples is a power far greater than the atomic bomb.

What it all means is that the people of the United States must understand their role in the world more distinctly and accurately, and live up to it. Such understanding is manifestly a task of education and of communication, at all possible levels. We must revise, retain, revitalize the deepest values of our society. Our greatest source of strength, of course, is that we have a society based on respect for individual man. But such a society must solve the problems of living and working together. The collective problem is just as important as the individual one. And even a society with the ineffable advantages of individualism and freedom is not constructive and effective unless its goals and standards are sound and good. Welfare, both individual and collective, must be accurately defined. It must contribute to the true well-being of people.

It is very healthy that education is engaged in a process of self-examination. All our institutions should be similarly probed. And the study should not be defensive. Our society was never so strong as when it was most open to the impact of criticism and the inflow of new ideas. I am not competent

to discuss the relative merits of Soviet and American education. I would not seek to insert into our society the dour
and doctrinaire disciplines of Marxist life as led in the
U.S.S.R. I would not sacrifice the humanities on the altar
of a technological state. I would preserve the breadth and
balance and freedom of all that is good in Western education. But every one of our practices and assumptions should
stand the test of re-evaluation.

Yet, as I said at the beginning, the fault is not within our
institutions but within ourselves. That is where re-examina-
tion, and understanding, must begin. So let me affirm that
the abundance of our economy, the richness of our life, the
immense new capacity of man to solve the problems imposed by material conditions—all these things and many
more are not the product of materialism. They are the result
of man's God-given capacity to think, plan, organize, achieve.
They are in reality triumphs of the spirit. Distorted and
abused, these new achievements of man may be made to
serve mammon. They can delude us into a preoccupation
with goods instead of with good.

In the global conflict of symbols, the loincloth is not
necessarily good, and the tail fin is not necessarily bad. There
is nothing inherently unspiritual about a pair of shoes. In
the war for the minds of men, the abundance of goods is at
once an advantage and a handicap. If we see abundance not
as an end in itself, but as a means of enriching the content
of lives, and if we act as if we knew this truth, there is
some chance of winning the war. For men everywhere in the
underdeveloped world are eager for their chance to improve
their way of life—to reduce infant mortality, to improve
literacy, to get enough to eat. The awakening peoples do not

want to make themselves over into our model. Their ideals and aspirations must be their own. Their ways of attaining their goals—governmentally, economically, socially—must be consistent with their capacity, experience, and purpose.

Nevertheless, much in our experience can be helpful to all the others. And we can still learn a great deal from them. Thus the process of education and of communication can proceed—a two-way process. It is not complete unless the flow is in both directions.

So let us look deep within ourselves and find out what it is we have to say. Let us listen awhile. Then let us say it—and live with it.

PHYSICAL AND BIOLOGICAL SCIENCES
AND TECHNOLOGY

POLYKARP KUSCH
Professor of Physics, Columbia University

Physical Science —
Present and Future

IT IS, I THINK, appropriate to this occasion to look at the various disciplined activities of the human mind in the light of their historical development and their present status to try to determine their future directions and the role they will play in the affairs of men. I am, of course, aware of the hazards of prophecy, even of its absurdity. Had a physicist been brash enough to discuss the future of physical science on the occasion of the founding of this university nearly a century ago, he would have been very far indeed from a description of what has actually been learned and discovered within the last century. He might have predicted with some accuracy the continuing development of what we now call classical physics to the very high degree of perfection that it achieved by the end of the nineteenth century. He might have predicted the development of a technology based on the knowledge that physics was to bring. It would not have been unreasonable to predict flight in heavier-than-air

machines, the distribution of electric power, the development
of the automobile, the increasing availability of power. To be
sure, some of these things would have been foreseen only
with a considerable audacity; still, all these things have been
achieved through the extension and utilization of ideas and
knowledge that were current a century ago.

It is not conceivable to me that the physicist of a century
ago could have suggested the possibility of utilizing energy
produced by the conversion of mass into energy through a
nuclear process, and I use the most spectacular consequence
of our knowledge of nuclear physics only as an illustration
of the profound influence that the wholly unpredictable new
knowledge has had on our lives. I do not think that the
most imaginative physicist of a century ago would have
dreamed of the physical phenomena that are the basis of the
present science of electronics. The point is that prediction
always occurs within the intellectual climate of the prophet.
The really important changes that occur are those that grow
from wholly new knowledge, wholly unsuspected power. So,
with this awareness of the futility of prophecy, I shall still
discuss physical science with an eye to the future. I hope
that it may bring much more than I can now anticipate. Life
would certainly have been less exciting had the earnest
prophet of 1861 had a perfect vision of the future.

Classical physics had been brought to a high degree of
perfection by the end of the nineteenth century. I use the
words "classical physics" to describe the knowledge of the
macroscopic, large-scale world around us. In a spirit of self-
assurance quite foreign to contemporary physics (in spite of
what you may believe from personal knowledge of physicists),
it was thought that very nearly all of the basic laws that

govern the behavior of matter had been discovered. Only a careful and possibly difficult application of these laws appeared to be necessary to clarify all natural phenomena. While physicists of the time were certainly aware of the existence of atoms, they believed that an understanding of their behavior could be achieved within the framework of classical physics. The idea of the atomicity of matter is very old and can be traced back to Greek philosophical thought. Still, the physical theory at the end of the nineteenth century generally considered matter as a continuum. The detailed structure of the continuum, that is the atomicity of matter, neither was considered by such theory nor was it necessary in the formulation of physical law describing a large range of phenomena. Far from being a shortcoming of classical physics, it was a source of real power that the behavior of matter in bulk could be predicted with great precision without detailed knowledge of its structure.

Electromagnetic theory has had a brilliant success in describing magnetic and electric phenomena; indeed, one of the most important pieces of intellectual equipment of a creative electrical engineer today is still classical electromagnetic theory. This theory takes no cognizance at all of the fact that electrical charge occurs on the electrons and protons in matter, that the charge occurs in discrete units, and that the electrons and protons are constrained to move within matter in rather special ways. Classical thermodynamics, the science that deals with energy relationships within matter, makes no statements at all about the structure of the matter with which it deals; again, it is wonderfully useful not only as a device in the business of the power engineer and the chemical engineer, but as an intellectual construct that gives a penetrating understanding of many manifestations of nature. Classical optics had, at the end of the last century, become a special case of electromagnetic theory; it continues to be completely adequate in the understanding of a great range of optical phenomena and in the design and utilization of the optical instruments that are an important component of our modern science and technology. The macroscopic view of nature has, thus, been of inestimable value. It fathered the tremendous technological growth in the last century—the availability of power, of electrical devices, and of the products of the chemical engineering industry can all be traced to the success of the macroscopic view. What is more, the intellectual basis of a more sophisticated investigation of nature lay in the classical, macroscopic view.

At the end of the last century, surprising and qualitatively new phenomena were discovered. Among these phenomena were the photoelectric effect, radioactivity, and X-rays. It seems to me that there were good reasons why these phenomena had not been discovered earlier. The phenomena of radioactivity, for example, are not readily apparent to the unaided observer of nature. Rather, they require a sophisticated observational technique for their detection, and this was possible only with the devices that a technology based on classical physics had produced. Another prerequisite to the observation of the new phenomena was the skill and experience of the experimenter—that is, physics had evolved a theory of observation and measurement that was essential to the uncovering of obscure phenomena. X-rays, to be observed, must be produced in laboratory devices and could not have been discovered without the rather complex technology, based on a classical view, that was available to Roentgen in 1895.

It became evident that these and other new phenomena could not be brought within the framework of classical physics; indeed, the predictions of classical physics about these new phenomena were sometimes in flat contradiction to observation. From the vantage point of our present knowledge it is not surprising that the behavior of, say, individual atoms would not be predictable in all detail from generalizations derived from observations on aggregates of matter involving billions of billions of atoms.

The understanding of the new phenomena now recognized as those on an atomic scale required new statements, new laws of nature. It is particularly appropriate to mention Planck's quantum hypothesis, since physicists and others are this year celebrating the centenary of Planck's birth. The hypothesis essentially states that radiation exists not in a continuous way, but only as discrete units of radiation, or quanta, where each one of the quanta has a definite energy. The quanta of radiation are very small, and for many purposes we may consider their aggregate effect, but in discussing atomic phenomena we cannot do this since in a single atomic event only a single quantum is involved. Other new principles were stated: those of Bohr in giving the first satisfactory picture of the hydrogen atom; that of De Broglie, in ascribing wavelike properties to a particle; the statements of Einstein, most especially the best known of them, $E = mc^2$, which states that, in the annihilation of a mass m, an energy E is produced, where c is the velocity of light. All of the principles that were originally proposed on a rather *ad hoc* basis, to allow a tentative explanation of an ever-increasing number of phenomena on an atomic scale, were subsequently unified into a single magnificent conceptual structure, which we call the quantum theory. This was the work of many men. I shall mention only Heisenberg, Schrödinger, and Dirac.

The intellectual apparatus for dealing with atomic phenomena had been brought to a high state of perfection about twenty-five years ago and its essential validity demonstrated through countless experiments. The first thirty years of this century were exciting to all the participants in a quest for understanding of the atom. The new results were gratifying for they provided an extension of physics and not a negation of classical physics; that is, nothing in the quantum physics impaired the validity of classical physics in its own macroscopic area. To be sure, the new physics dealt less with intuitively appealing models than did the old physics. Rather, an abstract formalism was used in relating various observable manifestations of nature. While the classical mind recoiled, in many instances, from a theoretical structure all of whose details were not interpretable in readily visualizable terms, the new physics seemed to be perfectly reasonable to those who had not been so heavily indoctrinated in the classical view.

The knowledge of the nature and behavior of the atom has given us an enormous intellectual power. I personally believe that the highest manifestation of the human spirit lies in knowledge and understanding of the world within which man lives. To the extent that we have acquired profound insights into what is almost, but not quite, the ultimate building stone of matter, the atom, to that extent has man been enriched. The certainties of science are today less emphatic than they were a half century ago: first, because experience has shown how limited the insights of the physics of a half century ago have been, with the obvious lesson to the contemporary world; and, second, because the intellectual structure of modern physics itself is such that absolutes do not, in some senses, exist. The development of modern physics has, through this fact, had an important effect on philosophical thought.

The development of the physics of the first third of this century has had a profound effect on our physical as well as our intellectual lives. This is true for several reasons. The value of the methods of science had been so thoroughly demonstrated that even classical scientific thought was imaginatively put to new uses. There is nothing about the complex technology of television that could not have been mastered shortly after the discovery by J. J. Thompson of the electron in 1897. Nevertheless, it took the same surge of scientific thought and a related technological development to develop both our complex communication systems and our knowledge of atomic phenomena. The great ferment of scientific discovery was, thus, an essential ingredient of technological innovation.

But in addition to this the new physics has had a very specific effect on our technology. Our knowledge of many of the details of the structure of solids has been brought about by a prior knowledge of atomic phenomena. It is not conceivable to me that the detailed study that led to the discovery and application of the transistor principle would have been possible in a preatomic era. Our greatly increased knowledge of chemical compounds, often very complex and

useful ones, of their structure, properties, detection, manu-
facture, and so forth, is directly related to the microscopic
knowledge of nature that has been developed in the first
part of the century. The diagnostic and therapeutic use of
X-rays is the result of the new physics. A large number of
the tools of industry depend on phenomena unheard of at
the founding of this university and only dimly understood
when it was celebrating its first semicentennial.

The most remarkable thing that atomic physics brought
us was an awareness of the nucleus of the atom, if not a
detailed knowledge of its structure. I think that the physicist
of perhaps a quarter of a century ago may have believed that
the theory which described, so beautifully, atomic and molecular behavior could also be applied to describing and pre-
dicting the behavior of the atomic nucleus. This belief—not
often articulated, since physicists were aware that their
predecessors at the end of the nineteenth century had been
uncritically sanguine of the powers of classical physics—this
belief turned out to be quite unwarranted. In fact, inquiry
into nuclear behavior elicited knowledge about an entirely
new range of unanticipated phenomena. Up to a point the
physicist learned to deal with these phenomena. You in
Washington have been hosts to the Hanford Works long
enough to understand that we have indeed acquired knowledge about the nucleus and the power and ability to manipulate it. The intensive study of the physics of nuclei led to
still a new branch of physics, called high energy particle
physics. This concerns itself with mesons, hyperons—
generally strange particles in the sense that they had been
quite unsuspected when atomic theory itself had already been
beautifully perfected.

The point I am making is that intensive inquiry into one field points the way to new fields. The classical physics, itself a satisfying intellectual structure, allowed, because of the content of ideas and a technology fathered by it, concentrated inquiry into atomic phenomena. The perfected science of atomistics, again by virtue of its content of ideas and by virtue of techniques to which it gave birth, allowed an intensive concern with nuclear phenomena. An increasing knowledge of the nucleus revealed the world of strange particles.

I should not want you to believe that a great and all-pervading light now illuminates all the physical phenomena of nature. Science has learned a great deal about the nucleus—enough to extract energy from it and to transform it. But there is a very great gap in our knowledge of the nucleus—what forces hold it together, what possible combinations of neutrons and protons produce stable nuclei. Physics has a long way to go to achieve the kind of understanding of the nucleus that it has acquired of the atom. A great deal has been learned about the behavior of the new particles of physics, but the role these particles play in the structure and behavior of matter is still obscure. I think that new and fundamental knowledge about nuclei and particles is forthcoming, perhaps with any luck before your centennial but almost certainly before your sesquicentennial. A new set of ideas, the basis of a new conceptual structure, is required, just as a half century ago some basic and novel ideas, quite different from those of classical physics, were required to allow an attack on what appeared at that time to be the extremely difficult problems of atomic structure.

It has been said, correctly I think, that the quantum

mechanics contains all of chemistry within itself, that is, all basic knowledge of the interactions and reactions among molecules and atoms. Still, not even the most optimistic physicist would seriously maintain that laboratory research in chemistry is no longer necessary since we may now compute, more or less from dead reckoning, all properties of all molecules. The point is that the complexity of the application is so enormous that one cannot successfully apply the raw basic principles.

The flourishing science of the solid state is not likely to produce any new and really fundamental statements about nature. Most physicists would agree that all of the basic ideas are contained in the content of classical and quantum physics. Still, the problem of applying these ideas to the ensemble of a vast number of electrons and nuclei within the solid is, I think, hopeless of solution. An experimental approach to the study of solids is still essential if we are to understand the behavior of solids. From the experimental data, one may hope to find new generalizations, applicable to the system under study—generalizations of an experimentally determined validity, of a simplicity that makes their application useful and wholly consistent with the grand conceptual schemes of physics. None of this is to suggest that the basic laws are of no value; on the contrary they give important clues to the behavior of matter as studied by the chemist and the solid state physicist. The utility of the basic laws, perhaps of the framework of thought in which these are used, is indicated by the enormous increase in our knowledge of both chemistry and physics; neither chemistry nor the physics of solids could have proceeded as far, as rapidly, and as successfully as they have in this century without a basic understanding of quantum phenomena.

Let me recapitulate briefly. The basic problem of physical science is the problem of the atomic nucleus and the intimately related problem of strange particles. A great deal is known about both of these, but basic and universally applicable statements, certain fundamental laws, are yet to be found. Those phenomena of physics and of chemistry that are not concerned with the detailed structure of the nucleus probably do not require new basic conceptual schemes for their interpretation. Nevertheless, further generalizations, derived from experiment, are necessary to deal adequately, both on purely intellectual grounds and on the grounds of application to technological problems, with systems of any significant degree of complexity.

We have at our disposal a great storehouse of knowledge about nature; the knowledge is incomplete, difficult of application, and quite possibly not correct in all instances. It is the problem of technology to use this knowledge to improve the life of man on earth. Evidence of the effectiveness of technology is all around us. We have come here by automobile, train, and plane. Arrangements for this symposium have been made by telephone, telegraph, air mail, and, for all I know, teletype and television. The hall is at a comfortable temperature, the lighting is good, the amplifiers operate noiselessly. It is a remarkable tribute to our technology that we take all these things on faith. When I wrote this talk in New York a few weeks ago, I assumed, correctly, that all these products of technology would operate flawlessly to make this symposium possible.

Technology has not by any means exhausted the fund of basic knowledge in modifying the physical life of man. Phenomenal technological advances were made in the last war under military necessity. It is notable, however, that the advance of basic knowledge during the war was slight. I use this as an example to illustrate the point that an aggressive technology may go very far with present knowledge. The arts of chemical synthesis, of the production of new materials and perhaps of new foods, are in their infancy. I believe it to be not improbable that at some future time man may exist on earth without the intermediary of plant life to convert the energy of the sun and the lifeless material of the planet into sustenance for him. Indeed, the grave problems that rapidly increasing population levels present to society may well make the most pressing technological objective the conversion of the sun's energy and the inorganic material of the earth's crust and atmosphere into the materials that man needs. To be useful this process must, of course, be more efficient than nature's own process.

I think that we are just at the beginning of a rapidly increasing utilization of the remarkable properties that solids have. It would not, I think, have been guessed a quarter of a century ago that a triode amplifier could be made in which the essential element, the vacuum tube, could be replaced by a piece of rather ordinary-looking white metal to whose surface a few wires had been connected. I do not know what novel properties of solids may yet be found and what applications may be made of these properties, but I am quite certain that there will be new and ingenious applications of the properties of solids.

I think that the application of nuclear processes to the production of energy is in its infancy. We are accustomed, in this day, to expect technological advances to occur with great rapidity, and perhaps we are vaguely disappointed that there is not yet an aircraft propelled by nuclear power. Perhaps we think that we are losing our grip because a plant to produce electric power for New York City by the fusion process is not yet on the drawing board. The sudden onset of the atomic age has posed technical problems of unprecedented difficulty to the scientist and the engineer. New techniques need to be evolved and developed. I myself have no doubt at all that our technology will rise to the challenge of the nuclear age, and I believe that we *may*—and it is a big *may*—reap all the benefits that are, in principle, possible from our ability to modify the atomic nucleus.

Let me emphasize that there is nothing magical or wonder-working about science. The laws of nature, once they are understood, have what I will call a permissive quality, that is, they state what nature can do or can be made to do, what is in principle possible, and what technology may try to achieve. When Ernest Lawrence designed and built the first cyclotron he did not, of course, make a random assembly of magnet iron, wire, glass, vacuum tubes, and the other gear of physical research. There were very definite requirements that were imposed by nature—and once these were fulfilled there was a high probability of success. Similarly, the circuits that made television transmission and reception possible had a predictable behavior and were not random collections of circuit components. I am sometimes surprised to note the great range of possibilities that nature allows us, to note how an understanding of the basic elements of the operation of nature may point to quite novel and unexpected but still realistic technological possibilities.

The laws of nature also have an exclusive quality, that is, they indicate what cannot be done in principle and what is, therefore, fruitless for our technology to attempt. The classic case is that of perpetual motion. Within the usual definition of the term, I flatly assert that it is impossible. Sometimes well-meaning inventors are annoyed by this flat assertion, especially when it is made without a careful study of the blueprints for the perpetual-motion machine. One could think of all sorts of other proposals whose realization would be revolutionary in their effects but which have the fatal defect that they are wholly inconsistent with the known properties of nature. I am, thus, emphasizing the rationality of science. It cannot work miracles; in fact, it is a basic tenet of science that all manifestations of the physical universe conform to inviolable law.

Solutions to all the intriguing problems suggested by nature are not even remotely in sight. Let me mention just one. Generations of scientists have thought that it would be interesting, to say nothing of useful, to be able to manipulate gravitational forces. This seems to me to be an unattainable goal in the foreseeable future; it is not possible to assert that this will be either possible or impossible at any time.

Man has achieved increased stature as a civilized creature and increased dignity through the increase of his knowledge; he has been relieved of supersititon about nature and fear of it. To be sure, supersision has not been wholly banished; still, man's belief in the order and the predictability of nature has been greatly increased with the growth of knowledge.

The technology that has been fathered by science or, in some instances, that has fathered science has immeasurably improved the lot of man. He has been freed from backbreaking toil in large areas of the world; he may enjoy warmth, comfort, and safety. He may travel easily. He may read, thanks to printing, and he may read in comfort, thanks to the electric light. He may hear the Bach *B-Minor Mass* exactly when he wishes. The catalogue is indeed endless.

I have, I think, been optimistic, and correctly so, about the ability of science to acquire knowledge about the world and its behavior. I have been equally optimistic about the ability of technology to utilize the knowledge in producing devices and processes that will meet human needs, even presently unarticulated ones, as was, for example, the need of a telephone to Isaac Newton.

There are, however, conspicuous hazards that are associated not so much with the growth of science as with the technological devices made possible by scientific knowledge. The greatest and most conspicuous of these hazards is, of course, the unlimited destructive power that is available to man through the use of nuclear processes in bombs—not only the destructive power of a bomb with an explosive content equivalent to millions of tons of TNT, but the more insidious destruction associated with radioactive contamination of the earth, which may well affect man's survival as a biologic species. At the other end of the scale there is the hazard of the vulgarization of life, of the dull uniformization of human experience that some of the products of technology may bring—witness, for example, some of the worse horrors of television.

No human activity, no branch of inquiry that has a

demonstrable role in society as great as that which science and technology clearly have can proceed independent of the pressures of society. Ultimately it is society that accepts and utilizes the gifts of science. I take the position that science is neither good nor bad in itself, but that only the use to which society puts science is good or bad. Evidently, if we are to proceed to a brave new world we need not only knowledge of nature and the power to control and utilize it but wisdom as well. I am not a professional philosopher, and I would not attempt to give you a definition of wisdom. Still, there are certain qualities of the human mind and spirit that I would group together as the elements of wisdom. A knowledge of the nature of operation of the natural world around us is certainly one of them. But wisdom must also include a knowledge of man, of his history, of his aspirations, of the good life as viewed by present-day man and by his forebears. Wisdom must include the ability to make judgments of the values of the several kinds of human activity; it must include tolerance and urbanity, a sense of the nature of human society. It must see in the present organization and customs of society a phase in a continuous evolutionary process, not the final and glorious end of a long process. Wisdom must include, I think, a sense of beauty, a taste for it. Having got this far, I consulted Webster, who describes wisdom—ability to judge soundly and deal sagaciously with facts, especially as they deal with life and conduct; knowledge, with the capacity to make due use of it; perception of the best ends and the best means; discernment and judgment. Webster also says—scientific or philosophical knowledge; erudition; learning.

This brings me to the role of the university in a scientific and technological age. There is no more noble aspiration in human life than the increase of knowledge and the cultivation of skills to use the knowledge for valid human purposes. The status of man cannot be enhanced by ceasing to search for knowledge and by throttling the creative use of truth. It is, I think, an act of cowardice to avoid questioning and the search for answers in the fear that the answers may pose new hazards. It seems to me that vigorous scientific inquiry into nature and energetic application of scientific knowledge are essential if our civilization is to flourish and grow, even if it is to survive. Still, the truths of science and the skills of technology are far from the sum total of a civilized and enlightened society.

Note that I have used the phrase "valid human purposes" in a recent sentence, and the phrase "creative use of truth." Both of these phrases suggest a value judgment about human activity and, in the present context, about the uses to which scientific knowledge is put. It is, I think, the great need of the age to have educated and enlightened citizens make these value judgments. They must be made in the light of knowledge—perhaps understanding is the better word—of the external world of man, his history, his culture, the workings of his mind, and above all of the quality of the contemporary world, so heavily determined by science and technology.

I wish I could give a prescription for instilling wisdom into students and perhaps into the faculty as well. It seems quite certain to me that didactic instruction, however well-meant, will not produce the truly educated man, the man of wisdom. The organization of new curricula, new courses is not the answer either. New combinations of subject matter often proclaim a unity of knowledge where none in fact exists.

Still, the university must somehow or other meet the challenge if our world is to survive. Let me make a statement of a few prerequisites in meeting the challenge.

The university must be an institution dedicated to intellectual values—not to the values of the market place or the values determined by acclaim and applause. I mean intellectual in the broadest sense—an outlook on life in which rationality, judgment based on knowledge, is supreme. A vital intellectuality is not only something that is talked about, but something that lends its character to every aspect of the life of the institution; it must be contagious, that is, kindled by the faculty, nurtured by the administration, and felt by the students. The faculty must teach more than the dry bones of scholarship, though these have their uses. Wisdom is an interdisciplinary quality; no specialist has wisdom through the quality of being a specialist. The collected knowledge of specialists does not constitute wisdom either. Our earnest plans for truly educating our students—in wisdom, if you please—are almost certainly doomed to failure if they are carried out by collections of specialists. I totally disavow the intention of recommending the replacement of scholarly specialists by the broad-gauge man with a smattering of ignorance, a man who has never come to grips with hard intellectual problems. I do, however, argue that the specialist, a man of trained mind, a person of self-discipline, should undertake the program of educating himself first of all in the many aspects of human experience and perception not directly in his own field of scholarly competence. It seems to me that therein lies the first step on the road to the cultivation of wisdom within the university. Once this step has been taken the problem of education of the student within the university becomes, as one sometimes reads in mathematical treatises, obvious or, in any case, almost obvious.

Whether science in the present world will elevate the human spirit and the products of science will ennoble man, or whether they will lead to a destruction of life and of an environment in which life can flourish, and to the complete degradation of the human spirit, is the crucial issue of the age. The issue will be resolved by men; I myself will be much more optimistic of the future if the men who resolve the issue are men of wisdom; not scientists as such, not political scientists as such, but men who can deal sagaciously with knowledge. Therein lies, I think, the destiny of the university, its faculties and administration, to produce men of wisdom to aid in promoting the bright future that science offers us rather than in leading us to a sterile world of ashes.

MELVIN CALVIN
Director, Bio-organic Chemistry Group
Radiation Laboratory, University of California

Round Trip from Space

On such an occasion as this, the beginning of a new phase in the life of a university, we stop for a moment to review progress that men have made in their various fields of thought and action. One can choose a variety of ways of accomplishing this review. One could, for example, gather together and enumerate the specific accomplishments, both intellectual and material, in the areas of biology and chemistry. I have chosen, rather, to illuminate these accomplishments by seeking to answer a question that men have asked since first they thought, but to answer it particularly in the light of our progress in biology and chemistry in the last century.

The question of which I speak may be formulated in many ways. One way is to ask the question: Whence came life on the surface of the earth? Another would be, in more personal terms as Pearl Buck has asked it: "Who are we, by whom were we made, and how, and for what purpose?" Whether or not a complete answer to these questions may be found within the context, and content, of modern science remains a moot question.

It is my purpose this evening to see how far we can devise an answer, and how satisfactory it may be, within that context. It becomes clear immediately that we will be dealing with the advances that have occurred not only in biology but in all of the contiguous sciences—physics, chemistry, geology, astronomy, and the like. However, our primary point of view will be that of biology and chemistry.

In trying to provide this answer we will, of necessity, have to review the accomplishments, particularly of these areas, both in their practical, concrete knowledge as well as in the impact they have, and will have, on man's view of himself and his place in the universe. At every point of our discussion we will limit ourselves to asking questions and providing answers, which, at some point, may be susceptible of observational or experimental test.

WHAT IS LIFE?

Since we have phrased the question in terms of "the origin of life," we presumably have a clear conception of what we mean by the term "life." There is very little doubt that, on the ordinary level of human experience, there is no difficulty in distinguishing that which lives from that which does not. However, when we explore this notion to try to determine precisely what it is or, to be even more specific, what qualities we must devise in order to produce something that lives from something that does not with no help from a living agency save the hand of a man, the question becomes somewhat more ambiguous. For example, there are many qualities that we have no difficult in attributing to a living organism. It is able to reproduce itself, to respond to an environmental change (i.e., "come in out of the rain"), to transform energy into order (sunshine into a leaf, leaf into a hair), to change and remember the change, and so forth. While many of these individual characteristics may be duplicated in systems in space, one or more at a time, it is only when a sufficiently large collection of them appears in a single system in space that we call that system alive.

Thus, the definition of life takes on the arbitrariness of the definition of any particular point on a varying continuum, and precisely where that point will fall on the line of time and evolution will depend a good deal upon who is watching the unfolding of that line.

With this last remark we have introduced the basic notion of evolution, which, since its precise formulation exactly one hundred years ago by Darwin and Wallace, has pervaded all of science. In fact, most of what I have to say this evening could be formulated in terms of a long extrapolation backward in time of the notions that were so ably expressed by Darwin and Wallace in 1858, but which they did not extend very far back, either in geologic time or certainly in cosmic time.[1]

As most of you know, for a period of over sixty years any serious discussion of the question of the origin of life was not indulged in by scientists, particularly by experimental scientists. In fact, it was considered a disreputable kind of activity. It is interesting to examine what some of the reasons for this might have been. One, certainly (and perhaps a

[1] C. Darwin and A. R. Wallace, *Journal of the Proceedings of the Linnean Society, London* (Zoology), III (1858), 35-62.

dominant reason), was the dictum of a contemporary of Darwin (1809-82), a chemist, Louis Pasteur (1822-95), who, in 1864, quite clearly provided an answer to the question that for many decades before had been the subject of much discussion, namely, the possibility of the spontaneous generation of life on the earth today. Pasteur quite clearly and definitely established, in his experiments of 1864, that it was impossible on the earth today, under controlled conditions, to demonstrate the appearance of living material except through the agency, or as offspring of, other living material. While Pasteur opposed the Darwinian formulation of evolution, largely on religious grounds, I suspect that he either knew consciously, or felt instinctively, that the Darwinian doctrine was conceptually in conflict with his experimental conclusion.[2] A search of the works of Darwin has revealed no mention of his opinion of the conclusions that Pasteur reached in 1864.

In any case, for over sixty years thereafter, as I mentioned earlier, there appeared practically no serious discussion of the origin of life, or of spontaneous generation. Between the publication in 1870 by Alexander Winchell, a professor of geology, zoology, and botany at the University of Michigan, of a book entitled *Sketches of Creation*,[3] and the statements by J. B. S. Haldane, professor of biology, in 1928,[4] there appears to be no serious attempt to answer the question of the origin of life within the context of the science of the period.

[2] Paul Sears, *Charles Darwin* (New York: Charles Scribner's Sons, 1950).
[3] Alexander Winchell, *Sketches of Creation* (New York: Harper and Bros., 1870).
[4] "The Origins of Life," *New Biology*, No. 16 (1954), pp. 12-27.

The hiatus came to an end with the recognition, by Professor Haldane, that the dictum of Pasteur was not in conflict with the backward extrapolation of the doctrine of evolution as expounded by Darwin and Wallace if one recognizes that at the time that spontaneous generation must have occurred, according to the evolutionary extrapolation of Darwin and Wallace, there was not, by definition, any living thing on the surface of the earth. Therefore it was possible, in the prebiotic time, for large amounts of organic material generated by nonbiological processes to accumulate. This, of course, cannot take place on the surface of the earth today, since there exist everywhere on the earth's surface organisms, both micro- and macro-, which would transform any such organic material immediately it was formed, even in small amounts. Thus, the apparent conflict of concept between the backward extrapolation of evolution and the dictum of "no life save from life" can be, and has been, resolved.[5] Since that time, that is, 1928, it has become increasingly popular among scientists (experimental and otherwise) to examine the question of the origin of life from the scientific point of view. In fact, it has become so popular that within the last eighteen months there have been held at least two conferences in the United States and one international conference on the subject.

[5] A. I. Oparin, *The Origin of Life* (3rd ed.; London: Oliver and Boyd, 1957). See also L. Pauling and H. A. Itano (eds.), *Molecular Structure and Biological Specificity* (Publication No. 2 of the American Institute of Biological Sciences) (Washington, D.C., 1957).

THE TIME SCALE

It seems wise to have a look at the time we have in which to accomplish this total evolution of life. In the first of our figures (Fig. 1), we can see something of the order

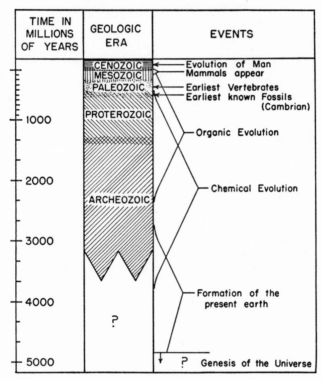

Fig. 1. The time scale for total evolution

of magnitude of the time with which we have to deal related to the geologic history of the earth. The earth was formed from matter in space some four to seven billion years ago. Whether this formation was an aggregation of cosmic dust or a primeval explosion remains a matter of some controversy and will come up again a bit later in our discussion. However, that terrestrial history itself is only some five billion years in extent seems to be well established. Figure 1 shows the evolutionary periods on the surface of the earth marked to correspond with the known geologic eras.

The earliest period might be spoken of as the period of the evolution of the present earth. Overlapping this, and including the Archeozoic and Proterozoic geologic eras (some four to two billion years ago), is the principal period of which we will speak, namely, the period of Chemical Evolution. It was during this time that the formation of more complex organic molecules from simple ones occurred by nonbiological methods that we shall try to describe below. Overlapping the period of Chemical Evolution we have marked the period of Organic Evolution, up to the present day. This period of Organic Evolution is the one whose later part is recorded in the form of fossils. However, for its greatest part, beginning some time in the Archeozoic period and extending through the Proterozoic period, there is no fossil record. This period of Organic Evolution of the soft-bodied living organisms, which left no fossils, constitutes by far the longer fraction of the period which we call Organic, or Biological, Evolution. Finally, at the very apex of the entire structure exists a point that we call the Evolution of Man. This constitutes only something like the last million years of geologic time, and it is clear that this represents a minute fraction of the time period with which we have to deal.

THE PRIMITIVE ATMOSPHERE

It should be noted that one of the prerequisites of all of the speculation about the origin of life is that there exist a means of gradually producing relatively complex organic substances by nonbiological processes. This question is susceptible of experimental investigation and has been investigated by a variety of experimental scientists, with positive results. It is clear that, in order to test any chemical process as a possible means of generating organic materials by nonbiological means, we must first know what the raw materials for these chemical processes must be. This, of course, entails some knowledge of the nature of the atmosphere of the primeval earth. This, in turn, requires a concept of the mode of formation of the earth and the solar system in which it exists. There have been a wide variety of hypotheses on this point. For example, Shapley, in his recent discussion, lists some fifteen different hypotheses with regard to the origin of the earth and the solar system.[6] In any case, one thing is common to all of the hypotheses, namely, that the earth did have a solid crust and some kind of gaseous atmosphere. The question that is open to some discussion is whether that crust and atmosphere were primarily oxidizing or primarily reducing in character. In the former case, the dominant partners for all the atoms are oxygen atoms, while in the latter they are hydrogen atoms.

It is clear that, no matter what concept one accepts for the origin of the earth, the atmosphere itself must have been

[6] Harlow Shapley, *Of Stars and Men* (Boston: Beacon Press, 1958); Fred Hoyle, *The Nature of the Universe* (New York: New American Library, 1955; first published in England in 1950).

made up of relatively simple molecules such as nitrogen, ammonia, possibly carbon dioxide, methane, hydrogen, and the like. A group of these molecules is shown in the first row of Figure 2. There has been considerable discussion as to

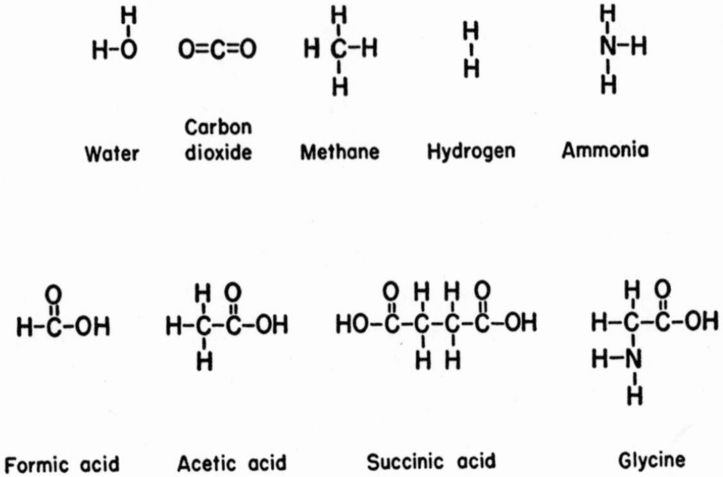

Fig. 2. Primeval and primitive organic molecules

whether the oxidized molecules or the reduced molecules constituted the major portion of this atmosphere. It would appear that the present consensus favors the reduced group. In any case, experiments have been done with both types of atmosphere.

RANDOM ORGANIC SYNTHESIS—
THE BEGINNING OF CHEMICAL EVOLUTION

The agents that have been called upon to produce the initial transformations have nearly all been of the high-energy type—ultraviolet radiation, electrical discharge, radiation from radioactivity of earth-bound minerals, or radiation coming from outer space in the form of cosmic rays.[7] Since it appears that all of the concepts of the earth's formation involve the absence of molecular oxygen from its primeval atmosphere, the intensity of ultraviolet light that impinged on the surface of the earth in its early days was considerably greater than it is today. Thus, some of the earliest experiments designed to determine whether more complex organic molecules, containing carbon-carbon bonds, could be formed were done using the ultraviolet light as the source of the energy. They were described by Haldane as early as 1928, and since then they have been checked in a variety of laboratories throughout the world. The primitive carbon compounds used in most of these experiments were already partly reduced, such as carbon monoxide, formic acid, or formaldehyde.[8]

In 1951, in our laboratory at Berkeley, experiments were again instituted to determine the usefulness of high-energy radiations, such as those which might be derived from the natural radioactive materials present in relatively high concentrations in the primitive earth, or from cosmic radiations coming in from space.[9] Here, the primitive carbon compounds were of the more oxidized type, strictly speaking, carbon dioxide. However, molecular hydrogen was also present in the experiments. The partial reduction of carbon from the completely oxidized form of carbon dioxide to a partly reduced form, such as formic acid or formaldehyde, was ob-

[7] Oparin, *The Origin of Life;* Pauling and Itano (eds.), *Molecular Structure and Biological Specificity.*

[8] Haldane, "The Origins of Life."

[9] W. M. Garrison, D. C. Morrison, J. G. Hamilton, A. A. Benson, and M. Calvin, *Science,* CXIV (1951), 416.

served. In addition, new carbon-carbon bonds were apparently formed upon irradiation of aqueous solutions of such carbon compounds, leading to compounds such as oxalic acid and acetic acid, shown in the second row of Figure 2.

Still more recently, beginning with the premise that the primeval atmosphere was of a reducing character, experiments were undertaken that were designed to test the effectiveness of electrical discharge in the upper atmosphere (a reduced atmosphere) to create materials more closely resembling those which are presently used in biological activities.[10] Here the compounds used as starting materials were water vapor, methane, ammonia, and hydrogen. As you see, these were primarily the reduced forms of each of the elements, that is, the elements of oxygen, nitrogen, carbon, attached only to hydrogen. When an electric discharge was passed through such a mixture, one did indeed get a large variety of more complex materials, particularly those known as amino acids, of which the simplest, glycine, is shown in the figure. It is perhaps worthwhile to point out that, having first reduced the one-carbon compound in the high-energy experiment and then formed a two-carbon compound by connecting two carbon atoms in the form of acetic acid, one could demonstrate the generation of succinic acid, a four-carbon compound, resulting from the combination of two molecules of acetic acid, by irradiation with high-energy radiations such as those one might obtain from radioactive materials. It is interesting to note that these latter experiments, as well as the first ones of 1951, were done using a cyclotron rather than natural

[10] S. L Miller, *Journal of the American Chemical Society,* LXXVII (1955), 2351.

sources of radioactivity because of the high intensities of ionizing radiation that could be obtained.

One suggestion of a very different type was among the early ones used, since the elementary chemistry was already well known. This chemistry begins with metallic carbides,[11] which, on contact with water, will produce a variety of hydrocarbons such as methane and acetylene (the latter the familiar process used in the older miner's lamp). Some of these gases are of such a character that, if they come into contact at high enough concentration with any of a variety of mineral surfaces, they will combine with each other to produce large, complex molecules, sometimes with very specific configurations.[12] The metal carbides used to start such a process generally require high temperatures for their formation, and it will therefore be necessary to suppose either that the earth began very hot or that it has had at least some places in, or on, it that were hot enough to form such carbides and later deliver them to the cooler surfaces. There appears to be no geologic evidence for the primary existence of such carbides in the deep rocks.

Very nearly all of these processes which we have just described for the generation of new carbon-carbon and carbon-nitrogen bonds and the creation of more complex molecules from simpler ones are processes that depend upon the primary disruption of the simple molecule into an active fragment, followed by the random combination of those active fragments

[11] Oparin, *The Origin of Life;* Pauling and Itano (eds.), *Molecular Structure and Biological Specificity.*

[12] G. Natta, "Stereospecific Catalysis and Stereoisomeric Polymers," speech at opening conference, XVI Congress of Pure and Applied Chemistry, Paris, July, 1957.

into something more complex. As the material present in the atmosphere and on the crust of the earth is gradually changed from the simple to the complex, these methods of transformation will not select between the simple and the complex and are just as prone to destroy by bond breakage the products of their initial activity as they are to create new ones. It is from here that we must now call upon some method of selective construction of molecules.

THE EVOLUTION OF CATALYSTS—ENZYMES

To do this we need only call upon the phenomenon of autocatalysis, well known to chemists.[13] This phenomenon occurs whenever the product of any chemical transformation has the property (catalytic) of influencing the rate of its own formation. It is somewhat surprising that this phenomenon was not long ago utilized in such discussions as these, since it is, in essence, the very fact and form of the mechanism of all selective evolutionary processes, namely, that selective superiority of any form to reproduce itself will give rise to a transformation of material into that particular form.

Thus, it is easily apparent from Figure 3 that, of three possible transformations that A might undergo, namely, to B, to C, or to D, it will undergo more frequently the transformation to D because D itself is a better catalyst for that transformation than it is for the others. Therefore, eventually the random processes that gave rise to A will not be quite so completely random in their further effectiveness. They will, in this case, tend to produce D rather than B or C from A. In general, the selective process of autocatalysis—in higher

[13] M. Calvin, *American Scientist*, XLIV (1956), 248.

evolution as well as in lower—is not an "all or none" process as we have described it, but rather one of a matter of degree. Thus, the actual situation is more likely to be that all three substances, B, C, and D, are catalysts for their own formation, but the most efficient is the one that will eventually supersede the others.

It is of interest to examine how this sort of chemical selectivity might have functioned in the development of an

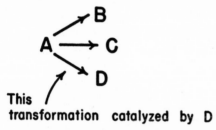

Fig. 3. Autocatalysis
as the means of chemical selection

extremely important biological material that is widely distributed today. This class of material is represented by that which gives the red color to blood cells and the green color to leaves. It constitutes a very important class of organic substances known by the name of porphyrins. We have already seen how the simple precursors to porphyrins, succinic acid and glycine, might be formed (and, indeed, were formed) by a random process from the primeval carbon-containing molecules. Now we have available to us a method of tracing the route by which these two precursors eventually become porphyrins in present-day living material, and some

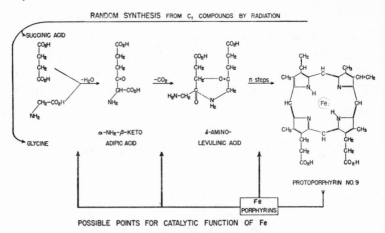

Fig. 4. Biosynthesis of porphyrin and the evolution of the catalytic functions of iron

of the essential steps in that series are shown in Figure 4.[14]

Underneath the center sequence are indicated, by arrows, a number of possible points where the catalytic function of iron might play a role. For example, iron may play a part in the combination of succinic acid and glycine to start with, or in the decarboxylation of the primarily formed keto adipic acid, which is the second compound in the center row, or, finally, in one of the several steps necessary to convert the delta-aminolevulinic acid into the macrocyclic, or large ring, compound known as protoporphyrin No. 9 at the right-hand end of the figure. We already know that a number of these steps are definitely catalyzed by iron, but what is more important is that some of them are much more readily induced to go by the iron ion after it has been encased in the porphyrin No. 9, as shown by the dotted circle in the porphyrin,

[14] D. Shemin, *Harvey Lectures*, L (1954-55), 258.

than they are by the bare iron ion. Such an iron porphyrin is a much better catalyst for several of the steps leading to its own formation than is the bare iron ion itself. Furthermore, it is almost certainly a better catalyst for the conversion of the levulinic acid toward the porphyrin than for the competitive conversion of the glycine back toward the carbon dioxide whence it came. Thus it is clear that the route from succinic acid and glycine to the porphyrin, once the porphyrin has been formed, will be greatly facilitated by the incorporation of iron into it, thus bringing a good deal more of the succinic acid and glycine into this particular, and important, form.

The process of the development of the catalytic function of iron does not and has not stopped at this point. When the iron compound is built into a protein (a macromolecule made by combination of many amino acids), its catalytic efficiency may be increased still more. Beyond this, the variety of chemical changes in which it may assist can be increased and the efficiency of its function diversified.

Other atoms and groups of atoms having rudimentary catalytic powers can be developed into the highly efficient and specific catalysts that we know as enzymes in even the simplest of modern organisms by exactly analogous processes of chemical selection by autocatalysis. And it is almost certainly no "accident" that these enzymes are all proteins. For it is only the proteins as a class that offer the combination of simplicity of formation (peptide bond) with practically an infinite variety of chemical function (R groups)[15] (Fig. 5).

[15] F. H. C. Crick, *Biological Replication of Macromolecules* (Society of Experimental Biology, Symposium XII) (Cambridge, Eng.: Cambridge University Press, 1958), p. 138.

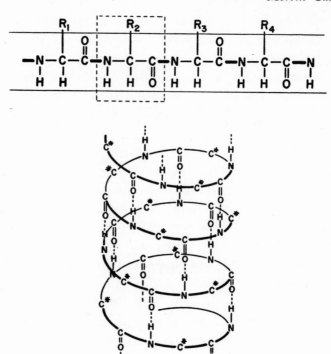

Fig. 5. Protein structure: simple structural principles and
variety of chemical reactivity

FROM CHAOS TO ORDER—
MOLECULAR CRYSTALLIZATION

So far, all the processes of which we have spoken have
been described as taking place in a rather dilute solution, with
the molecules randomly arranged. The development of a complex material under such circumstances could not go very far.
Two further stages of change seem to be required: (1) the
ordering of the molecules in some rather specific array, and

(2) the concentration of the formed substances into relatively small packages. Which of these two processes took place first, or whether they were indeed successive or simultaneous developments, is hard to say. However, that both of them took place we do know, and that there exist mechanisms for each of these processes to take place we can also demonstrate in the laboratory.

One type of molecule, for example, with which we are constantly dealing, both in the laboratory and as a result of present-day biological action, is the large, flat, so-called aromatic molecule. The porphyrin that we have just mentioned constitutes one such, and there are many others. Such molecules, when they reach a certain minimal level of concentration in aqueous solution, will tend to drop out of that aqueous solution. However, they will not drop out in a random way. Because of their peculiar flat shape, they will tend to drop out in an arrangement in which the molecules are piled one on top of the other, much like a pack of cards. If one throws a pack of cards in the air and allows them to fall out of the air onto the floor, it is unlikely that they will fall standing on edge. They will, of course, practically all (if not all) land flat, one on top of the other, because of their peculiar shape. This kind of phenomenon illustrates the way in which large, flat molecules tend to come out of solution in crystals. Figure 6 shows a diagrammatic drawing of a simple crystal of a rather simple flat molecule, and here you can see the results of the tendency of such molecules to pile up one on top of the other.[16]

[16] M. Calvin, Brookhaven National Laboratory Biology Conference, No. 11, in press; University of California Radiation Laboratory Report, UCRL-8411 (October, 1958).

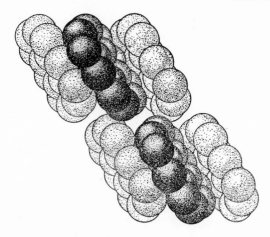

**A packing drawing of the anthracene
structure projected on its b face**

Fig. 6. Packing of flat molecules in a crystal

I use this particular type of example with a purpose in
mind. The reason is that much of the information that
present-day living organisms carry with them and can transmit to their offspring in the form of genetic material is made
up of, or seems to be contained in, an ordered array of such flat
molecules as these. The additional feature that one must
add to this piling-up of flat molecules is that they are not
independent, as the group of cards was, but that they are all
tied together along an edge, as though the group of cards
were tied together by a double string. The example of the flat
units that we will use here will be the pairs of complementary
bases as they are found in desoxynucleic acid (DNA), the
material of which the chromosomes are constructed. Figure
7 shows these pairs as they occur: thymine paired with

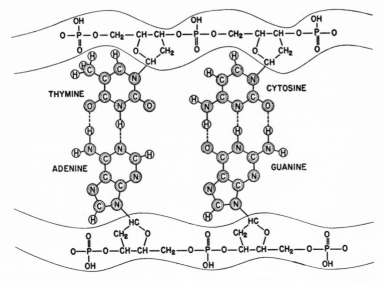

Fig. 7. Molecular drawing of the components of desoxynucleic acid—
genic material

adenine and cytosine paired with guanine by virtue of their
peculiar structure, which places certain of the hydrogen atoms
between oxygen and/or nitrogen atoms on the complementary
molecule. These four molecules, and one other very closely
related to thymine, are themselves formed from the same
primitive precursors described in Figure 2 (succinic acid,
glycine, formic acid, carbon dioxide, and ammonia). Along
either edge of these flat units you can see the sugar-phos-
phorus chain that corresponds to the string-card analogy I
spoke of a moment ago.

Because of their peculiar aromatic type of structure these
base pairs will tend to line up one above the other. This
tendency will, of course, be increased because they are not
independent of each other but tied together by the sugar-

phosphate ribbons. In actual fact, the structure of desoxynucleic acid (DNA) seems to be such a flat piling up of the nucleoside bases with the sugar-phosphate ribbons twisted in a spiral around the outside, as shown in Figure 8.

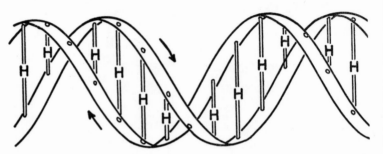

Fig. 8. Double helix model for desoxynucleic acid (DNA). Source: J. D. Watson and F. H. C. Crick, *Nature*, CLXXI (1953), 964.

CONCENTRATION AND LOCALIZATION— THE FORMATION OF A CELL

The other aspect of which we spoke a moment ago, which must obtain, is the concentration into relatively small volumes in space of these organic materials, leading ultimately to the formation of cells as we now know them as the units of living matter. It is at this point that our information and our analogies are most diffuse. However, a number of physical-chemical processes have been called on to participate in the development of the living cell. First among these is the appearance of surface layers or boundary layers, such as one sees in a soap bubble. Here we are quite familiar with mechanisms for producing a relatively stable and well-defined boundary layer between two phases. Another phenomenon that is much less familiar to us is known by the name of coacervation and has been called upon as a primary phenomenon leading to the development of local concentration and cellular structures.[17] This phenomenon is dependent upon the ability of giant molecules in water solution to separate out from the dilute water solution into relatively more concentrated phases, or droplets, suspended in the more dilute water solution around them. Beyond this, the giant molecules tend to pack themselves in ordered arrays, provided that they, themselves, have ordered structures.

While the knowledge of the interaction of giant, or macro-, molecules, both synthetic and natural, has made great strides in the last decade or two, we are still only at the beginning of our investigation of systems of macromolecules of sufficient complexity to provide us with the kind of information we would like to have for the present purposes. However, it seems to me that already enough information is available for us to be able to say with confidence that the basic kinds of physical-chemical processes upon which we shall have to draw in order to describe the evolution of the cellular structure are already at hand.

THE SELECTION OF THE PILOT—DNA

That characteristic which is most frequently invoked as the prime attribute of living material is the ability to reproduce and mutate. Very frequently, in discussions of the origin of life, attempts are made to define that certain point in time before which no life existed and after which we may speak of "living" things, as that point at which an or-

[17] Oparin, *The Origin of Life;* Pauling and Itano (eds.) *Molecular Structure and Biological Specificity.*

ganic unit, be it a molecule or something bigger, came into
existence that could generate itself from existing precursors
and that could sustain and propagate a structural change.
Since we can be confident that genetic information is transmitted today in the environment of a cell by the chemical
substance known as desoxynucleic acid (DNA), of which
we have already spoken, it seems reasonable to seek in this
structure the clues to the mutable self-reproducing molecule,
or unit.[18]

It should be pointed out that, while we are in the habit
of thinking of the nucleoprotein molecules that constitute
the chromosomes and viruses (DNA and RNA, ribonucleic
acid) as containing all the information required to produce
its entire organism, this is not strictly true. These structures
may be said to contain information only in relation to, and
exhibitable through, a proper environment. Thus, it is possible to keep a bottle containing only virus particles (say
DNA) indefinitely, just like any other organic chemical,
and the question of whether it is alive or not would not
arise. The moment these particles find themselves in a
suitable organic medium (such as may be found in any
of a variety of cell cytoplasms), this information makes itself
apparent and the virus multiplies. There are thus other
constituents in the modern cell which contain indispensable
information but under direction of the nucleoprotein of the
chromosomes.

While a mechanical model [19] operating in one dimension

[18] J. D. Watson and F. H. C. Crick, *Nature*, CLXXI (1953),
964.
[19] L. S. Penrose and R. Penrose, *Nature*, CLXXIX (1957), 1183.

has been described which is able to control the behavior of a mixture of precursor units as it goes on to form a larger material, it is only in recent months that the ability to separate the controlling information-carrying units from the energy-transforming units and to demonstrate that information can indeed be carried by the desoxynucleic acid particles has been achieved.[20]

You will recall that the DNA, or chromosomal material, is made up of a linear array of only four units, represented in Figure 7 by the four bases (adenine, thymine, cytosine, and guanine), and that the controlling information about the organism (at least a modern post-Cambrian cell) is contained in some kind of linear array of these units. In the past few years it has been possible to isolate from various living organisms, particularly bacteria, a catalyst (enzyme), which, when placed into a solution containing all four of these units in an active form, that is, as their triphosphates, was able to induce their combination into some particular linear array of bases to produce a particular variety of desoxynucleic acid. Which particular DNA was formed depended entirely upon the presence of a very small amount of so-called "starter," which had to be added to this mixture. If this starter was obtained from one type of cell, that particular type of desoxynucleic acid would be formed; if it was ob-

[20] M. J. Bessman, I. R. Lehman, J. Adler, S. B. Zimmerman, E. S. Simms, and A. Kornberg, *Proceedings of the National Academy of Science*, XLIV (1958), 633; J. Adler, I. R. Lehman, M. J. Bessman, E. S. Simms, and A. Kornberg, *ibid.*, p. 641; A. Kornberg, Abstracts of 134th National Meeting of the American Chemical Society, Chicago, Illinois, 1958, Abstract No. 21C; M. Grunberg-Manago, P. J. Ortiz, and S. Ochoa, *Science*, CXXII (1955), 907.

tained from some other type of cell, another type of DNA would appear.[21]

Still more recently, it has been possible to make a synthetic desoxynucleic acid consisting of only two of these bases, in particular the thymine and adenine.[22] This synthetic DNA presumably has no counterpart in nature today, and yet, when this synthetic material is given as a "starter" to the reaction mixture, as previously described, that particular two-base desoxynucleic acid, made up of only thymine and adenine, is produced. The catalyst that is able to do this seems to be the proteinlike material constructed of amino acids in the way proteins usually are. Although little is yet known about the nature of this catalyst (enzyme), it will almost certainly be related to the simpler compounds and elements whose more primitive catalytic abilities constitute the basis for its action. This is exactly analogous to the relationship between the catalytic ability of simple iron ions and that of the highly effective iron proteins, as described in Figure 4.

We have thus traced a path from the primitive molecules of the primeval earth's atmosphere, through the random formation of more or less complex organic molecules, using the available energy sources of ultraviolet light, ionizing radiation, or atmospheric electrical discharge, through the selective formation of complex organic molecules via autocatalysis, finally to the information-transmitting molecule

[21] S. R. Kornberg, I. R. Lehman, M. J. Bessman, E. S. Simms, and A. Kornberg, *Journal of Biological Chemistry*, CCXXXIII (1958), 159; I. R. Lehman, M. J. Bessman, E. S. Simms, and A. Kornberg, *ibid.*, p. 163; M. J. Bessman, I. R. Lehman, E. S. Simms, and A. Kornberg, *ibid.*, p. 171.
[22] H. K. Schachman, private communication.

that is capable of self-reproduction and variation. During the course of this process we have, naturally, made use of the organic materials that have been produced in high-energy form via these various energy-yielding routes. In addition, somewhere, either during the course of this Chemical Evolution or perhaps succeeding it, a system was evolved in which the concentration of the reaction materials was retained in a relatively small volume of space, leading to the formation of cellular structures.

PLOTTING THE COURSE—
BIOSYNTHETIC PATHWAYS

During this entire course we have made use of the randomly formed molecules, followed by a chemical kind of selection. The ultimate production of the information-carrying molecules depended upon the preformed presence of their constituent units, for example, nucleoside triphosphates or "active" amino acids. It is clear that, as the efficiency of transformation is increased by chemical or early biotic evolution, all of these precursors will have been used up, and a mechanism will have to be devised for the regeneration of these precursors by more specific chemical routes than those originally used. We can see these very specific biosynthetic routes in the living organisms of today.

The last ten to twenty years, since the application of tracer techniques particularly, have exposed to us the wide variety of relatively complex biosynthetic sequences, an illustration of which we had in Figure 4 leading to the porphyrin, and which appear to be a sequence of reactions directed toward a particular end. The usefulness of any intermediate step does not become apparent until the final product is formed. Such sequences, on an organismic level, have led to a variety of teleological theories about the nature of evolution. However, on the molecular level it is possible to see the way in which complex, apparently directed biosynthetic sequences arose by the operation of the ordinary laws of physics and chemistry, including the idea of autocatalysis as the basis of selection.

This was pointed out by Horowitz some years ago when he recognized that, once having formed a useful material into an "organism," which could transmit its information to its offspring, this process would continue so long as precursors were available for this "organism" to use for its reproduction.[23] However, eventually it was clear that one or another of these precursors would become exhausted. That particular organism which could adapt itself by a random variation to make the missing precursor from molecules that still remained available to it would, of course, survive, provided the knowledge of how it was done could be transmitted; all the others would die out. Thus, we would not have lengthened the chain of synthesis by one step, but in a backward direction toward the simpler precursors. By extrapolating this back, eventually, to carbon dioxide, one can get the very complex and what appear to be totally directed syntheses from the very simplest of all carbon compounds.

THE ULTIMATE FUEL—PHOTOSYNTHESIS

We have remaining one additional attribute that is always associated with living material and that is very fre-

[23] N. Horowitz, *Proceedings of the National Academy of Science,* XXXI (1945), 153.

quently called upon as a prerequisite to life, namely, the ability to use energy-yielding chemical reactions to create order out of disorder. Ultimately, of course, the large-scale evolution of living organisms to the extent that we are now familiar with it could not take place until the invention of photosynthesis, that is, the coupling of the ability of certain molecules to absorb solar energy to the ability of certain other molecules to use this energy for the synthesis of the necessary structures. Here is it almost certain that the ability to synthesize had been evolved long before the ability to couple the absorbed solar energy to those synthetic reactions was discovered. The use of porphyrins by nonphotosynthetic organisms is widespread, and almost certainly random variation in structure led to the discovery that small changes in the porphyrins, leading to the construction of chlorophyll and its use in transmitting energy for biosynthesis, led to the invention of photosynthesis.[24]

Strictly speaking, the primitive synthesis of which we spoke, making use of ultraviolet light or ionizing radiation, is a form of photosynthesis, and in all probability there existed a parallel evolutionary development of this kind of energy conversion process. In fact, modern work by physical chemists[25] on the effect of the far ultraviolet light on some of the simple molecules we spoke of earlier as constituting the primitive atmosphere of the earth has demonstrated experimentally the feasibility of the idea of the conversion of water (H_2O) into hydrogen (H_2) and oxygen (O_2). It has even been possible to demonstrate the conversion of carbon

[24] M. Calvin, University of California Radiation Laboratory Report, UCRL-3915 (August, 1957).
[25] R. G. W. Norrish, Liversidge Lecture, *Proceedings of the Chemical Society, London* (September, 1958), p. 247.

dioxide (CO_2) into carbon monoxide (CO) and oxygen (O_2) by the use of sunlight of such a high energy that very little of it penetrates down very far into the present earth's atmosphere.[26]

Whether the conjunction of the use of visible light-absorbing substances, such as the porphyrins, with the biosynthetic demands of the more highly evolved chemical systems took place before or after the appearance of what we would today call living organisms matters little for the purposes of our present discussion, important though the question may be. It seems quite clear, however, that these two parallel lines of development did meet, as mentioned earlier, giving rise to the very efficient energy conversion processes resembling those we know today. It is not unlikely that the final step in the development of modern photosynthesis, namely, the evolution of oxygen, did not take place until relatively late in the sequence of events. For example, we do have organisms today that are capable of using solar energy, via the agency of porphyrin-type molecules, but using other methods of taking care of the oxygen by combination with suitable reducing agents such as hydrogen. These appear in the form of photo-reducing organisms such as the photosynthetic bacteria. They dispose of the oxidizing fragment of the water molecule, made by the absorption of light, by combining it with whatever reducing materials may have been present in the primitive atmosphere. It is not until the higher green plants appear that we find the ability to dispose of this oxygen back into the atmosphere as molecular oxygen.

[26] Bruce Mahan, private communication.

THE FOSSIL RECORD—MAN'S PLACE

With this biological discovery the stage was set for the enormous development of living organisms on the surface of the earth as we know them today. From here on the fossil record is quite complete, and there is little point in our pursuing in detail the ascent and divergence of life, leading ultimately to mankind in the last million years.[27]

It is perhaps worthwhile at this point to try to assess the amount of time that may be allotted to each of the major kinds of operations, or sequences of events, that we have outlined as leading ultimately to cellular life as we know it on the earth today, and to man. It is a matter of general knowledge that from the very beginning the fossil record contains evidence of very nearly all of the major subkingdoms, or phyla, of life today. This fossil record, which is some five hundred to one thousand million years old, thus indicates that by the time life was sufficiently well developed to leave a fossil record it had already manifested itself in very nearly all of the major types of forms which we now recognize. This time period constitutes something less than one-quarter of the entire habitable life span of the earth. Thus we have some two or three billions of years during which we can pursue the process of Chemical Evolution, overlapping with that part of the evolution of cellular life (biotic evolution) which was unable to leave a record of itself in the rocks. This is an

[27] G. G. Simpson, *Meaning of Evolution* (New Haven, Conn.: Yale University Press, 1950). Also T. Dobzhansky, *Evolution, Genetics and Man* (New York: John Wiley and Sons, 1955).

extremely long period of time, which gives ample opportunity
for the enormous numbers of trials and errors that would be
required to develop all the possible molecular processes and
combinations that must have been tried.

Undoubtedly many different information-carrying molecular species had a birth, a life span, and a death, much as
we now see in the fossil record for the higher forms. One
(DNA), or only a few, of these closely related, information-
carrying molecules, or molecular species, eventually superseded all the rest, because of the particular structural, chemical, and dynamic properties of this arrangement of atoms,
i.e., stability, template or complementarity quality, mutability,
and others as yet not defined. It was from this—or these—
that the present-day organisms have developed, thus providing a basic similarity in all living processes as we know
them today.

The determinism in the arrangement of a system increases
with the number of trials (events) that can occur in reach-
ing it. On the molecular level, where the number of changes
occurring per second is high, predictability with regard to
what will happen in a given situation to a group of molecules amounts to certainty. For example, pressure main-
tained by bombardment of molecules on the walls of a vessel
containing a certain number of gas molecules at a specified
temperature is quite predictable. While we cannot specify
the particular molecules that will strike the wall at any
time, we can be quite sure that in a given period of time
a certain number will do so.

At the other extreme, the segregation and recombination
of genes that may take place in the formation of a new individual by (geologically) modern genetic mechanisms ap-

pear as a completely undetermined, or random, choice, since only a single event is involved. However, among a group of organisms of a given species there will be a predictable distribution of properties at a given time under a specified set of conditions.

On the other hand, coming up from molecules and molecular aggregates, we will reach a stage, probably after the invention of cellular heredity based on nucleic acid, when the number of events (rate multiplied by time available) will not be large enough to insure that all arrangements possible will have been tried, and an indeterminism with respect to those that have appeared will ensue.

Therefore, while an indeterminism exists with respect to the character of any individual living thing, and a limited indeterminism exists with respect to species, the time element is so great, and the amount of genetic material that has been cycled through the sequence of birth, growth, development, and death is so enormous,[28] that the certainty of the occurrence of cellular life as we know it on the earth today seems assured, given the initial starting conditions.

A most convincing demonstration that such a sequence of events, leading from nonliving matter to life, could, and probably did, take place, would be an experiment in which a system of organic material, called alive by most biologists, is produced through the agency of no other life save the hand of man.[29] And already today there is serious discussion as to whether some of the experiments performed in the last year might not fulfill these conditions.

[28] C. P. Swanson, *Cytology and Genetics* (Englewood Cliffs, N.J.: Prentice-Hall, 1957), chap. xii.
[29] H. Reichenbach, *The Rise of Scientific Philosophy* (Berkeley, Calif.: University of California Press, 1951), p. 202.

It thus appears that man is a rather late and highly developed (perhaps the most highly developed) form of that organization of matter which we call living, on the surface of the earth, and which is the result of the peculiar and special environmental situation provided on the surface of the earth since its formation some five billion years ago. We have known for some time now that the earth is the number three planet in orbit around a rather ordinary star on the edge of one of the minor galaxies of the universe. Thus, presuming life to be a unique occurrence limited to the surface of this one rather trivial (in terms of mass, energy, position, and so forth) planet in the universe, man, though an impressive representative of the state of matter called living, is not viewed as a major cosmic force.

LIFE ON OTHER PLANETS?—
A COSMIC INFLUENCE

Now man is about to send back into space some bits of the dust from which it originally came. This return will be in the form of machines, and eventually of man himself. It is thus not only timely but more significant than ever before to ask again the question: What are the probabilities that cellular life as we know it may exist at other sites in the universe than the surface of the earth? In view of the chemistry of carbon (and a few of its near neighbors) and the consequences this has given rise to in the environment to be found on the surface of the earth, all that is required to answer—or to provide some kind of answer to—this question is an estimate of the number of other sites, or planets, in the universe that might have the environmental conditions within the range to support cellular life as we know it on the surface of the earth.

Here we follow Shapley (as well as others),[30] who begins his calculation with an estimate of the minimum number of stars that might be in the universe. His minimum calculation, based upon the best telescopes we have today, is of the order of 10^{20}, that is, one with twenty zeros after it. The next step is to determine what fraction of these stars will have a planetary system. To make this estimate one must have some concept of how our planetary system was generated. Here there are many theories, and Shapley lists fourteen or fifteen of them. However, there are a number of conditions that must be fulfilled, and these, taken together with the fact that the universe has been expanding, and that some five billion years ago when the planetary systems were formed the universe must have been much more crowded than it is today, give the figure of one in a thousand as a very conservative estimate of the number of stars that have a planetary system.

The next question Shapley attempts to answer is what fraction of these planetary systems will contain a planet at approximately the correct distance from its star such that it will have a temperature variation compatible with the cellular life that we are seeking to determine. Here, again, we arrive at the very small, and what we consider conservative, figure of only one of these planetary systems in a thousand as containing a planet at approximately the right distance from its sun. The next circumstance that must be fulfilled is that of size. Again, the planet must be of the correct size to retain an atmosphere and not be too large. Here Shapley gives the

[30] Shapley, *Of Stars and Men*; Hoyle, *The Nature of the Universe*.

figure of one in a thousand as a conservatively small fraction.

Finally, of all these planets that are the correct size, which of them will have the proper atmosphere, containing carbon, hydrogen, nitrogen, and oxygen, that will be required to give rise to cellular life as we know it on earth? The answer is, again, the very conservative number of only one in a thousand.

Thus, we have four factors of one-thousandth by which we must multiply our figure of 10^{20} (the minimum number of stars that might be in the universe). This leads to the number 10^8, that is, one hundred million, as the number of habitable planets to be found in the universe. Remember that this calculation is limited to those planets that will have conditions within the range compatible with cellular life, based on carbon, as we know it on earth. This does not include systems, which conceivably we can imagine, based on other elements, such as silicon, or nitrogen, or perhaps even on antimatter. Such worlds and such systems may very well exist. However, these are not included as possibilities in this calculation. We have already cut down the limits by our four factors of one-thousandth, leading to something of the order of one hundred million planets that can support cellular life as we know it on the surface of the earth.

Since the time element seems to be about the same for all parts of the universe, namely, something greater than five billion years, it would appear that we can be reasonably certain that these hundred million other planets will indeed have cellular life on them. Since in the course of the chemical and biotic evolution the appearance of man on the surface of the earth has occupied only a very small fragment of time, namely, only one million years of the five billion, it is clear that we may expect to find cellular life, and perhaps precellular life and posthuman life, in many of these other planets. The one-million-year period given to the evolution of man on earth constitutes an extremely small element of this long period of time, and an uncertainty of this order could, and almost certainly does, exist in the status of the evolutionary sequence elsewhere in the universe.

We can thus assert with some degree of scientific confidence that cellular life as we know it on the surface of the earth does exist in some millions of other sites in the universe. This does not deny the possibility of the existence of still other forms of matter, which might be called living, which are foreign to our present experience.

By answering our second question in this way, we have now removed life from the limited place it occupied a moment ago, as a rather special and unique event on one of the minor planets around an ordinary sun at the edge of one of the minor galaxies in the universe, to a state of matter widely distributed throughout the universe. This change induces us to re-examine the status of life on the surface of the earth. In doing so we find that life on the surface of the earth is not a passive, existing thing, but actually changes and forms the environment in which it grows. The surface of the earth has indeed been completely transformed in its character by the development of the state of organization of matter which we call life. Furthermore, it is undergoing another, and perhaps a more profound, transformation by one representative or manifestation of that organization of matter, mankind.

MAN IN SPACE—THE NEXT STEP

Now that man has the capability of taking his machines and himself off the surface of the earth, and of beginning to explore outer space, there is no reason to suppose that life, and man as its representative, will not transform any planet, or any other astral body upon which he lands, in the same way, and perhaps in an even more profound way, than he has transformed the surface of the earth. For example, it might suit him in the future to change the course of the orbit of the moon, and it seems within the realm of possibility that he should be able to do so. When we realize that other organisms may be doing similar things in some millions of other regions in the universe, we see that life itself becomes a cosmic influence of significant proportions, and man, as one representative of that state of organization of matter, becomes a specific cosmic influence himself. Thus have we come to a complete inversion of our view of the place of life and of man in the universe from a trivial to a major cosmic influence. And we have come to this view entirely upon the basis of experimental and observational science and scientific probability.

Man's adventure into space, which is about to begin, is not merely a flexing of muscles—a demonstration of strength. It is a necessary aspect of evolution and of human evolution in particular. It is an activity within the capability of this complex organism, man, and it must be explored as every other potentially useful evolutionary possibility has been. The whole evolutionary process depends upon each organism's developing to the greatest extent every potential. It is the par-

ticular function of the university to facilitate this development of the uniquely human potential of understanding and
control—to lead the species in its new exploration rather
than only to serve it in transmitting its established patterns.[31]

[31] For general references on evolution see *Evolution* (Society of
Experimental Biology, Symposium VIII) (Cambridge, Eng.: Cam-
bridge University Press, 1953), particularly article by J. W. S.
Pringle on "The Origin of Life"; Julian Huxley, *Evolution in
Action* (New York: Harper and Bros., 1955); H. F. Blum, *Time's
Arrow and Evolution* (2nd ed.; Princeton, N.J.: Princeton University
Press, 1953).

THE HUMANITIES
IN THE MODERN WORLD

ARTHUR S. P. WOODHOUSE
Head, Department of English
University of Toronto

The Place of Literature in the Humanities

IT IS, I HOPE, unnecessary to assure you that the title of this paper is an honest title and not a thin disguise for an oration in praise of literature. My aim is to be as nearly objective as possible, and I would avoid even the appearance of advancing my own discipline in competition with any other. There is an old quarrel, for example, between philosophy and literature. I shall not renew it, but shall try instead to discover their common ground and their differences, and shall perhaps lay, on behalf of literature, a modest claim to some share in the philosopher's interest and in the historian's, too.

If we can satisfactorily define "the humanities" and "literature," and can reach a measure of agreement on the educational results to be expected from them, we shall have gone a long way toward answering the question of the place of literature in the humanities; and I will make no apology for organizing my paper around this basic problem of definition.

III

I

The humanities, then, is the name currently given to a group of disciplines embracing the languages, their literatures, the fine arts other than literature (these arts being relatively late-comers to the academic scene), philosophy (at least over a substantial part of its large territory), and finally history, which claims a dual classification in the humanities and the social sciences.

Historically, this grouping of disciplines is not difficult to explain; for (with the exception of the fine arts) they cover the subject matter once included under some such general heading as *litterae humaniores*—the principal subject matter of liberal education for Cicero, and for the Renaissance and subsequent centuries. It was an essentially literary education, and it was of course classical, finding all that it required of language and literature, of philosophy and history, in the writings of ancient Greece and Rome. Since the Renaissance, and especially in the last century and a half, there have been two important developments in the humanities: the extension of content to include the rich achievement first of the modern Western world and now of the Orient; and the elaboration and differentiation of techniques of study, with the attendant breaking away of the various disciplines to form separate departments (and even subdepartments such as archeology, not specified in our list). In the course of this development some part of some disciplines broke away from the humanities altogether to form a new category, the social sciences, but in most of them a sense, more or less unquestioned, of belonging to the humanities remained—of being indeed the differentiated offspring of *litterae humaniores*, that is, of literature, broadly conceived.

So far the history of the humanities will carry us. Nor does it entirely fail us when we come to the reason for the grouping and for the common name. At least it supplies us with four facts of which something may be made.

First, the etymology of the term "humanities" unmistakably roots them in the life of man, his experience and achievements; and as we turn back to our list of disciplines we see at a glance that each of them meets with ease this requirement. But the criterion is quite inadequate by itself to differentiate the humanities from other disciplines, and especially from the group of more recent organization, the social sciences, which also center upon the life of man, his experiences and achievements, only qualifying the range of their interests by the adjective "social." Here, indeed, an arbitrary line of demarcation has suggested itself but must, I think, be summarily rejected since it would confine the humanities to a consideration of man as an isolated individual, a restriction historically indefensible and philosophically absurd, for man is by nature a social being and all the disciplines of the humanities have always recognized that fact.

The operative distinction lies rather in the word "science," deliberately chosen by the social sciences to indicate their adoption of a descriptive and, where possible, a statistical method borrowed from the natural sciences. Even here the distinction is not complete, since in the investigation of language, in the amassing of historical evidence, and perhaps in other divisions of the humanities, scientific method has a place. But language is the *art* of expression as well as a body of existing phenomena, and history is an art even if it rests on a scientific collection and criticism of evidence. Indeed of the humanities at large it may be asserted that they cannot rest content with the method of science but must share, in varying degree, in the modes of thought and means of expression that are the peculiar property of art. And this is a second fact that can be verified in the history of the humanities.

A third fact emerges from their history, commencing once more with the term itself. At least as early as the fifteenth century, "humanity" (in the singular, as translating *humanitas*) was used to designate secular studies, and especially the classics, as distinguished from divinity. To distinguish, of course, is not necessarily to separate, as Coleridge reminds us, and as the long history of Christian Humanism would confirm. The distinction is valid, however, and important; but, if it is to be used to define the area of the humanities, there must be a corresponding distinction to establish a second boundary—a distinction between the study of man and of the rest of nature. Not that the humanities imply commitment to Humanism in any one of its various meanings. All they demand is the recognition of an area of study distinguished from theology on the one hand and natural science on the other, and a study pursuing its own ends and employing appropriate means.

Fourth, on the question of ends and means the history of the humanities throws some light. In the Latin of Cicero, *humanitas* signified the qualities, feelings, and behavior proper to mankind and was not descriptive only, but normative in function; and it came further to connote, in particular, intellectual cultivation. Thus *humanitas* defined the end of liberal education; and the word and its cognates, coupled with *litterae* or *studium,* designated the appropriate subject matter, which for Cicero was literature in its widest extent, including poetry, oratory, philosophy, and history. Times have changed, and science and the social sciences have claimed their due place in the educational scheme; but of the major groupings of disciplines only the humanities avows as its *sole* purpose that general cultivation of mind and sensibility which was the traditional end of liberal education.

We are deluding ourselves if we imagine that this end, and the role of the humanities in achieving it, is always accurately understood even by those engaged in education. There are some who regard the humanities as the merely ornamental subjects, and who think that their use is to impart a little superficial polish to what are often very rough diamonds indeed. There are others who seize on the notion (true enough if properly understood) that the humanities are concerned with values, and who would hasten to ally them with religion or alternatively would expect them to supply a sort of secular substitute for it. There are those, again, who would direct the humanities to particular tasks, such as the expounding, defending, and commending of our Western values, or on the other hand the deliberate fostering of international sympathy and understanding. Some excuse for these and other mistaken views, and for the short cuts they invite, may be found in the multifarious and pressing needs of our civilization; but this does not alter the fact that they are mistaken. They are mistaken because they forget that the humanities taken together constitute one of the great divisions of knowledge, and the division whose subject matter is nothing less than man in his specifically human aspect and aspirations; that this knowledge demands and deserves impartial critical study; and that the penetrative power of the humanities, their peculiar aptness to cultivate the mind and sensibility, depends wholly upon the character of their subject matter and not at all upon indoctrination undertaken in connection with them, which is indeed ruinous to their proper educational effect. This is not the despised doctrine of the ivory tower, but the plainest psychological realism.

By the modern educationist in a hurry, the humanities are often reproached for drawing so much of their subject matter from the past, the implication being that they are out of touch with the world today and indifferent to it. In this indictment are implicit, I think, two mistakes. The first is a mistake of fact. The history of the humanities during the past century and a half shows a steady appropriation of modern subject matter. But it is not a question of subject matter alone. No one who has studied and taught one of the humanities for any considerable time, or who knows the history of his subject, can fail to recognize the constant change in method and emphasis wrought by recent knowledge and contemporary modes of thought. The second mistake is to overlook an important function of the humanities, and of the humanities almost alone, in the larger strategy of education and culture. This function is the perpetuation of the tradition, and such a mediation of the past to the present as will enable the modern man to take secure possession of his cultural inheritance.

I have allowed myself to express some of my most deeply held convictions about the humanities, but I do not think that the issues raised are irrelevant to the special role of literature in the humanities, to which we must now briefly turn.

II

Again we may start with current usage, which at once reveals that "literature" has a wider and a narrower meaning. I do not refer of course to the vulgar usage that talks about "campaign literature," "advertising literature," and the like, and that the *OED* records as "colloquial," neatly supported by a quotation: "posters . . . and what by a profane perversion of language is called 'literature.'" I refer only to meanings that assume some criterion of value.

In its wider meaning "literature" includes all such writings as are addressed to the general reader and reach a certain degree (that is, a recognized, though undefined, degree) of significance in content and distinction in style. The definition is wide enough to embrace what De Quincey called the literature of knowledge: it will include the classics of history and criticism, and a surprising number of the classics of philosophy, of science, and of other subjects—all of Plato, much of Aristotle, most of the modern philosophers before Kant, and some after him, such as John Stuart Mill and William James; it will include *The Wealth of Nations, The Origin of Species,* Newman's *Apologia pro vita sua,* and hundreds of other works, which may be susceptible of more exact treatment by the philosopher, the economist, the scientist, or the theologian, but are still open to the general reader and negotiable as literature. It is on the basis of this wide definition of literature that the project of education by means of great books is based; and all of us are engaged on this project—at

least in the attempt to educate ourselves. In this view literature becomes one of the great meeting places of the various
disciplines, not only those within the humanities but those
beyond them.

In its narrower definition, "literature" is very nearly synony-
mous with what Aristotle called poetry, and De Quincey the
literature of power. It is an imaginative representation of
reality, with its own distinctive structure, capable of arous-
ing emotion, and achieving its end in pleasure. Today, no
doubt, we should wish to extend the definition to include
works that were representational only remotely if at all, to
make more provision for symbolic meanings, to couple with
structure esthetic pattern, and so to interpret pleasure as to
throw the emphasis at once on heightened awareness and on
esthetic satisfaction. But for our purpose of distinguishing
between the two meanings of "literature," the Aristotelian
definition of poetry, that is, of pure or creative literature, will
serve.

Thus conceived, literature is one of the arts—the art whose
medium is words; and this means that both as art and as
discipline it has affinities, on the one hand, with language,
and, on the other, with its sister arts. Like the other media,
the medium of words makes available special resources and
imposes special limitations. The qualities of structure and
pattern available to the other arts are likewise available to
literature so far (and only so far) as they can be realized in
words. Too obvious to be more than mentioned are the special
resources of literature for drama, for narration, and for description, which the other arts can achieve only by suggestion
and in a metaphorical sense, precisely as literature can paint
scenes, or produce musical effects, only in a metaphorical

sense. To its medium, words, literature also owes access to the whole range of verbal image and metaphor, on which current poetic theory lays so much emphasis. Less often noticed now, or given its full weight, is the opportunity opened to literature by its medium for the direct formulation of ideas, for supplementing representation by comment, and in extreme cases by an argument. Nor does the possibility stop here: the author can give to appropriate characters assumptions, speculations, and judgments, true or false, sound or unsound, and thus invite critical thought from the reader. It is this power of words that lends weight to Matthew Arnold's confessedly incomplete definition of literature as "a criticism of life by minds alive and active in extraordinary degree and at an extraordinary number of points." And it gives to literature one more affinity—with philosophy this time, or at least with abstract and speculative thought. Or, to put the matter in more general terms, literature, even when considered as a fine art, enjoys this common ground with the main body of the humanities: its medium, like theirs, is words.

In the earlier history of the humanities, the wider meaning of literature (as we have observed) prevailed: *litterae humaniores* were in fact the (as yet) undifferentiated humanities. With their differentiation, literature in the narrower sense became the primary concern of the discipline of that name. And it is a sufficiently wide and rich area. Besides multiplication of examples in the three genres of epic, tragedy, and comedy on which attention centered in Aristotle's day, new genres have been added, such as the novel, which has affinities with all three, and there has been so great a growth of other genres and subgenres, and of works that bridge the kinds, as virtually to force the abandonment of the genre as a method of classification, though it remains a useful point of reference. Romanticism added a whole new range of effects; naturalism, another; and later movements with their emphasis on myth and image, metaphor and symbol, yet more. The area of literature in its narrow sense, that is, as a fine art, is not only rich, but of almost bewildering variety.

Pre-eminent among its riches are the established classics, the works, said Longinus, that are capable of pleasing everyone, everywhere, always. Capable, that is, if they meet in the reader a corresponding capacity, and to evoke and refine this capacity is a principal function of literature as a discipline. The method, as in the other disciplines, is one of rigorous intellectual inquiry: its immediate aim, in a phrase that has never been bettered, "to see the object as in itself it really is." But thus to see the classic is to realize that here truth meets with beauty and with power, here significant content is united with significant form. What starts as an intellectual inquiry ends, if it is successful, in an experience of unique educative value, since it exercises our intellect and our sympathies, and probably our moral, and certainly our esthetic, perceptions: in a word, it exercises and augments our humanity.

Besides its educational value to the individual, the experience we have just described is one of the ways in which literature discharges that general function allotted to the humanities, the mediation of the past to the present, the preservation of the tradition as a vital part of our consciousness; and it does this so effectively because in the process one of the great achievements of the past becomes vividly present to us.

If the old question is impatiently repeated, this time in the form, "But are there, then, no classics in contemporary literature whose study is equally profitable?" the answer is that there are, of course, no *established* classics, but there are, or may well be, works of equal potency or perfection that admit to a similar experience, though an experience with different terms of reference and some different secondary benefits; nor is their (as yet) unestablished rank a serious handicap to the mature student—indeed it may well be an added advantage if it invites the fresh application of whatever standards he has been able to attain.

Up to this point we have been speaking as if the sole concern of literary study were the great classics or potential classics; and it is true that they hold a commanding place in the discipline. But many of the works of literature available for study fall below this high standard and yield the unique experience only partially or in inferior degree. They share with the great works a historical interest (in which term I include current as well as past history), but, unlike them, they do not go much beyond it.

Literary history is, however, one of the major concerns of literature as a discipline. The need for it, and the deficiency in it, were first remarked by Bacon. For no man, he writes, "hath propounded to himself the general state of learning to be described and represented from age to age . . . without which the history of the world seemeth to me to be as the statue of Polyphemus with his eye out, that part being wanting which doth most show the spirit and life of the person." This in the *Advancement of Learning;* and resuming the subject in the *De augmentis,* Bacon adds a word on scope and method. The literary historian, he says, must go to the "principal books written in each century or perhaps in shorter periods" and give some account of their contents, "argument, style, and method," simply "relating the fact historically with little intermixture of private judgment," so that "the literary spirit of each age may be charmed as it were from the dead."

We observe that Bacon is speaking of literature in its widest extent. He is doing so because humane letters had not yet been broken down into their respective disciplines: history and philosophy were still parts of literature. But we may appropriately follow his example since, where the primary interest is historical, the distinction between a narrower and a wider definition of literature is much less significant. His counsel of objectivity is as valid today as it was when he uttered it, and so is his perception of the hiatus left in general history if the history of literature is ignored. In its historical studies, literature as a discipline reaffirms its affinity with one more discipline in the humanities, namely, with history: it reaffirms its affinity, but not its identity. For literary history is not, generally speaking, the work of the historian who has turned his attention to the evidence that literature supplies: it requires a basic training in the study of literature itself and relies on the interests, perceptions, and skills which that kind of training best cultivates.

There is good reason for dividing the vast domain of literature, as in the modern university, between the major languages, since literature, unlike its sister arts, has no universal language of its own; and thus divided, furthermore, its manifold and varied examples become manageable. Their number and variety are greatly augmented if literature in its wider meaning is taken to fall within the scope of the discipline. That it should do so is the result of historical development but has its own propriety and some attendant advantages.

With the division of *litterae humaniores* into distinct disciplines, each assumed the portions of those studies which fell most immediately within its strict definition and submitted them to an increasingly rigorous treatment. Literature as a discipline has done precisely this with literature as a fine art, while language, philosophy, and history have pursued their own appropriate lines. But a degree of overlapping has testified to the continuing unity of the humanities. History as a method has proved applicable to all the disciplines. Philosophy, in addition to its special subject matter, has retained some interest in the theory of every discipline and in the coordination of their results. It is not surprising, then, that literature as a discipline should manifest a similar tendency. Thus it has taken possession, though by no means exclusive possession, of a large body of writings, some of which might also come under the cognizance of other disciplines, while some would be unlikely to do so. These writings are classics in their way, but certainly not works of pure art. Nor, on the other hand, are they directed exclusively to the advancement of knowledge in its more technical aspects. But they are patently part of the humanities, for their major preoccupation is the relating of knowledge in some particular field to the life and interests of man, and to man as such, that is, to the general reader, they are addressed. They reach a certain level of significance in content and effectiveness in expression. Their end is knowledge of a kind, not pleasure, but they can be read with pleasure—that is, with heightened interest and with satisfaction, which is, however, rather intellectual than esthetic. In short, they belong to what can be best described as the literature of knowledge and thus fall within the definition of literature in its wider sense. And gradually, and with increasing assurance, literature as a discipline has taken them under its special protection. They, in turn, have strengthened the intellectual content of the discipline and have helped to give it its large share in the more recent interdisciplinary activity, the history of ideas.

This inclusiveness is, then, one of the marks of literature as a discipline, and it is, of course, an inheritance from *litterae humaniores* as originally conceived. It enables the discipline to exploit to the full its natural affinities with all the other humanities. In its purest form and highest examples, literature gives access to the world of art and of esthetic experience, but to art as it works with and through words. Thus literature receives light from the study of language—receives light and gives it back. But literature shares its medium with philosophy and history. It has free access to the world of ideas and, even in its purest form, can invoke them and weave them into its patterns. From history it receives light whenever a work is considered in its setting, and once more the benefit is reciprocal—if Bacon was correct, and the writing of any period, present or past, "doth most show the spirit and the life." Finally, literature, by definition, addresses itself to the general reader. In a sense it meets him on his own ground, and therefrom it initiates him into an experience, intellectual or esthetic or both, of which he is capable, but which without its aid he would not enjoy. At the same time literature and the experiences to which it gives rise are susceptible of systematic examination. And it is these two facts that give to literature as a study its penetrative power and determine its role in the general strategy of education and culture today.

GEORGE BOAS
Professor Emeritus of Philosophy
Johns Hopkins University

A Task
for the Humanities

Pᴿᴼᶠᴱˢˢᴼᴿˢ ᴼᶠ the humanities are in a great tizzy nowadays. They see the scientists getting all the money, research grants, big fellowships, government contracts, and of course large salaries. They are told that students are drifting away from them to enter the natural and the social sciences. They seem to have the feeling that their work goes by the board and that they are becoming vestigial organs on the body academic. As far as the facts go, there is a good bit of truth in this. Whether it is something to be deplored is another question. But if humanistic studies are becoming obsolete, one might at least ask why.

One answer might well be that the professors of the humanities are killing their subject. As I read scholarly articles on the various literatures, I sometimes wonder what possible human interest they can satisfy. The search for sources and influences, one is glad to say, has become unfashionable, not because it is foolish to ask who influenced whom, but be-

cause there is very little left to do in the field. The discovery
of the exact date on which a given work appeared, the deriva-
tion of such words as "father" and "mother" from their pri-
mordial Indo-European roots, the tracing of fictional themes
from the folk lore of the ancient Aryans to the modern Germans, the collation of all the manuscripts of the *Romaunt of
the Rose,* a comparative study of the thirty-eight *Amphitryon*'s
are to be sure extremely important in their way, but their
way is the road that leads to pedantry. May I say that pedantry
is the solving of obsolete problems? What then is an obsolete
problem?

Problems may become obsolete for the following reasons.
(1) Like the squaring of the circle, they are seen to be in-
soluble. The most famous examples of this in literature are
the song the Sirens sang and the name Achilles assumed
when he hid among the women. (2) Like the discovery of
the position and velocity of a quantum of energy, they are
discovered to be meaningless. I should give as my pet example
of a meaningless problem in the humanities the discovery of
a *Zeitgeist.* (3) They are found to arise because of certain
assumptions that are no longer held. The calculation of the
epicycles of planets would be a good scientific example; the
seat of the soul, the distinction between white and black
magic, the unity of the arts would be good humanistic examples. (4) They go out of style. Nor must this fourth reason
be considered trivial. The role that great men play in history
is neither meaningless, nor theoretically undiscoverable, nor
implicated in abandoned assumptions. It has simply become
less interesting to historians than other problems. It happens
to be stylish nowadays to play down the contributions of in-

dividuals to history in favor of what are called great socio-economic laws. I suppose it runs parallel to a movement in painting that rejects the depiction of human beings, even in portraiture, for lines of force, masses in tension, the dynamic interplay of colors, and other things that are felt rather than seen.

Besides the obsolescence of many of our problems, we must confess to their narrowness as well. When a prospective doctor of philosophy in, let us say, French takes as his field of study the edition of a single French farce of the sixteenth century, or a *confrère* in English devotes his life to John Taylor the Water Poet, or a potential philosopher gives over his most productive years to contrary-to-fact conditionals, I am flatly saying that they have narrowed their targets to the vanishing point. The reply usually is that each of us is a tiny polyp building up a coral reef that will some day rise above the level of the sea. This is a very charming metaphor, if somewhat worn, and if it comforts anyone to compare himself to a polyp, I shan't deprive him of that pleasure. But the brains and industry, or perhaps I should say "assiduity," required for that kind of work could much better be put to solving some problems of greater importance to human welfare. Every problem, I suppose, is of some importance to somebody, but the present day confronts the humanist with problems of importance to almost everybody. And, if they are not, that is due to what I can only think of as intellectual laziness disguised as humility.

Since I have spent my life working in philosophy, I shall orient what I have to say in the direction of my former colleagues, though I shall not hesitate to take sideswipes at others.

If we measure the importance of a problem by the number of people whose lives it affects, one might choose as the most important the growth of authoritarianism. Authoritarianism has grown in the political field wherever totalitarian governments have taken over. It has spread in religion even in Protestant circles, where it is known as Fundamentalism. In schools and colleges it appears in standardized textbooks and courses, so that subjects as sheaves of problems not yet solved are supplanted by subjects to which the answers are known. Even in a democracy like our own, government has become more and more centralized in Washington, with the result that, even though regional differences may give rise to local problems, these problems will be handled by the federal government. The one place where authoritarianism has not got a firm hold is in the arts. But with radio, television, and national magazines whose circulation goes into the millions, the artistic individualist, if noticed at all, is noticed as a queer fish and little more. The prestige of an authority has become so great that men like Einstein or Schweitzer or Frank Lloyd Wright have been induced to give their opinions on all sorts of matters whether they are in their special domains or not.

The scientists as scientists can do little to combat this trend, for their subjects usually lend themselves to yes and no answers. It is of course not quite so simple as that, but nevertheless the sciences have perfected methods admirably adapted to analyzing their problems and solving them. But the humanities are quite different. There is no one right answer, as far as I can see, to such questions as, What is the meaning of *Hamlet*? *Hamlet* happens to be a work of art, and works of art contain many values and have as many meanings as there are kinds of people who see them, read them, listen to them. Is *Hamlet* a play about chivalric revenge, about the conflict between thought and action, about the Oedipus complex, about the Danish succession, or is it *about* anything? For all I know, it may well be about all these things and many more, and it also may be self-contained and refer to nothing beyond itself. What is a tree about, or a human being, or a landscape? "No one," says the late Joyce Cary in his very illuminating lectures, *Art and Reality*, "has ever seen the *Hamlet* that Shakespeare wrote and that the Elizabethans enjoyed. No one, in fact, reads the same book or sees the same picture twice." [1] This is, if not obvious, pretty nearly so. But it has been almost completely overlooked. Reading a book is interpretation, and every man is his own interpreter, and he can make his interpretation only on the basis of what he already knows and has experienced. The same remarks hold good of pictures. What is the "Resurrection" of Piero della Francesca? Is it a simple picture of a man rising from his tomb? Is it, as Sir Kenneth Clark seems to think, a symbol of the god of vegetation emerging from winter's death in the spring? Is it a pattern of certain shapes on a flat surface? I doubt that Piero himself would have agreed with Sir Kenneth, but then Piero had not had the advantage of reading *The Golden Bough*. Anyway his ideas about the painting need not be ours. The painting remains alive because it can stimulate a sensitive observer to make a new interpretation of it. Is the *Saint Matthew Passion* what is known as pure music; is the music an intensification of the text; is the whole an operatic version of an historical event; do the musical figures have a symbolic meaning of their own; are they conventional

[1] Joyce Cary, *Art and Realities* (Cambridge, Eng.: Cambridge University Press, 1958), p. 82.

early eighteenth-century arabesques; are they a perfect expression of the baroque in music? To such questions there can be no one answer in the nature of the case, for several of these questions could be answered in the affirmative without contradiction. As for philosophy, it is composed, as William James once said, precisely of all the questions that have not as yet been solved.

For a student to learn that there are such questions and that they are not the least important is, I cannot but believe, a great experience. During the Second World War, I was in command of a small group of Seabees who were operating in Brittany. One night an alarm was sounded, and we were told that the Germans had broken out of the pocket at Quiberon. I went with a captain of the F.F.I. to a listening post in the woods to get what information I could. For reasons I need not dwell upon, we recognized each other as civilians in uniform, and we talked about what we did when not engaged in warfare. When I told him that I was a teacher of philosophy, he said to me, "I have always admired philosophers since I studied the subject in the *lycée* at Rennes. For you philosophers see questions where we others see only facts." That is the best characterization of philosophy I have ever heard, though it does not describe all teachers of philosophy.

There would be nothing for the inquiring mind to do if all were known. There would be no need for academic freedom, for freedom of conscience, for freedom of speech. We might be willing to let a man believe that he could square the circle or invent a perpetual motion machine; but we would not let him teach mathematics or physics. If, however, all answers are not already known but on the contrary there is still room for inquiry, then it is essential that we encourage people to have their doubts, to criticize, to make their own interpretations, and to sneer at authorities. To perceive the narcotic effect of authoritarianism one has only to study the history of science and see for oneself the grip of the dead hand. The *"ipse dixit"* of the Pythagoreans, however, could easily be matched by the *"philosophus dixit"* of the Scholastics. But that is no worse than the "T. S. Eliot *dixit"* of our literary critics or the "Picasso *dixit"* of the art critics. Mr. Eliot is no doubt as great a critic as he is a poet; I am not here to say. Picasso is certainly a very great painter. But that they should be set up as standards of what we should think and do in the realm of esthetics is nonsense. They are just two people, two flesh and blood mortals, who will sooner or later be outdated and embalmed in histories of literature and painting. One of the best weapons against authoritarianism is a study of the history of any humanistic subject. For it would show a student, if the professor were willing to help, a vivid picture of the flux of opinion, of the human mind, like Whitman's spider, ceaselessly venturing, ceaselessly throwing, seeking the spheres to connect them. And, unlike the spider, not succeeding.

This by a natural association of ideas leads over to what I feel is the second most important problem of our time, the elimination of provincialism. This task cannot be accomplished by the sciences since they must be admitted to be largely a product of the Occident. There have been and still are eminent Oriental scientists, but the scientific tradition grew up in the West and has had its greatest hold there on the public imagination. The result usually is that natural scientists, even when they are acquainted with Oriental art and religion, seem incapable of taking any other attitude toward

knowledge than that of experimental science. Our sympathy
for the cultures of the East has come about through the
efforts of art historians, amateurs to begin with, and as early as
the eighteenth century through philosophers, who seem to
have been the first Europeans to appreciate the civilizations
of China and India. Missionaries, on the other hand, saw
very little to be praised in what they could understand only
as heathen rites, though the first Catholic missionaries to
China had a different story to tell. But when one studies the
various arts, literary and pictorial, the various philosophies
and histories of different peoples, one cannot escape the conclusion that individuality and difference are more striking
than universality and homogeneity. I realize that we have a
love of unity, though we seldom define the concept, and we
often strive to iron out the differences between, for instance,
two tragedies, two kinds of architecture, two systems of meta-
physics, but such attempts are usually futile, though, if one
ascends to an abstract enough level, everything is the same.

Fortunately there has never been developed a ritual for the
humanistic studies as compulsive as that which has the scientists in its grip. There have been schools of critics and
historians as there have been schools of artists. But it requires no great erudition to discover that each school usually
has lit upon some aspect of the arts or of history or of philosophy that remains significant. For instance, though impres-
sionistic criticism in matters esthetic has gone out of style,
nevertheless the pleasure one gets from reading or looking at
pictures is not to be laughed out of court. If reading a book
is no more than a painful duty to scholarship, no one is going to bother with it after he has got his degree.

In the case of the scientists, the method of Aristotle's

physics is no longer of interest to anyone but the humanist. No physicist is going to return to the theory of the four elements, natural position, the circular motion of the planets, and the attractive force of the Unmoved Mover. But to the historian these things are of importance since they illuminate the workings of one of the most influential minds in Occidental civilization and in doing so demonstrate how scientific theory may fit in with a whole philosophical system, a system including politics, ethics, esthetics, psychology, and biology.

This sort of thing may degenerate into antiquarianism and pedantry, but I am looking at its more valuable manifestations. The very fact that a scientific theory can be superseded even when it has been elaborated by an extremely able mind is itself something for the philosopher to note down. Aristotelianism did not collapse because of inner inconsistencies— though there were some in it—but because new questions were asked of nature and new instruments devised for answering them. Moreover, new demands were made upon science, pre-eminent among which was the demand for the control of nature. Hence, where the scientist quite properly discards theories that have outlived their usefulness, the humanist retains them if only as evidence that the human mind does change in spite of our hymns to unity and eternality. When the mutability of knowledge is grasped and absorbed into one's way of thinking, a new insight has been obtained into our lot on earth, and no one any longer can act as if he believed that he was the whole human race.

In that direction lies the escape from provincialism as I see things. And to have escaped from it is to have gained a new sympathy with different cultures and a new appreciation of one's own. Moreover, it gives one a new conception of truth as that which fits into a set of ideas accepted for reasons that do not lie within the domain of the subject in question but come into it from almost any other field. There is nothing but lack of time to prevent a scientist from asking humanistic questions, and many of them have asked them. But a humanist is not doing his job if he does not ask them. It seems important, for instance, to know how theological preconceptions determined the premises of science for several generations, if it merely induces one to ask oneself what determines one's own premises.

Let me cite just one example. For centuries the answer to the word "Why?" was a set of purposes. In biological matters that is sometimes still the answer. The scientists who were looking for purposive explanations were not fools, were not any less intelligent than we, but they envisioned a universe different from ours. Why are we satisfied when we discover the necessary and sufficient conditions for an occurrence? Is it because we have some revelations from the Holy Spirit telling us that such are the right and proper answers to our questions? Not at all. It is because we are all children of Francis Bacon, whether we are proud of our ancestry or not, and we want power over the course of events, and we can get it only by knowing the necessary and sufficient conditions for the occurrence of the events we want to produce. A scientist need not worry his head over the historical roots of his method. But it would seem that for a humanist to neglect such investigations would be for him to neglect one of his major problems. For, if he is not interested in intellectual development, what in the world is he interested in?

There is a third contribution the humanities can make that is frequently overlooked. What progress we have attained has come from dissatisfaction. A mind that is content with what it knows obviously will never look further for something more. Intellectual history will show, I think, that every once in a while a growing feeling of dissatisfaction appears until it finally culminates in someone's asking a question the answer to which upsets a large body of knowledge. This may occur in both the sciences and the humanities. For instance, in the eighteenth century we begin to find people dissatisfied with the notion of species, a notion that goes back to Plato and is incorporated in our common nouns. Every common noun names a species, and it has usually been assumed that such words are univalent. Behind this lies the assumption that species or kinds or classes—it makes very little difference which word one uses—are fixed and immutable. But, when men began to suspect for a variety of reasons that the concept was no longer viable, they began to examine species of things and found of course an impressive variety of traits within the species, and finally the term became a name for a large collection of things that were pretty much alike. We know what happened in biology because of this. But the same sort of thing began to happen in the arts, and by now I doubt whether anyone, except certain estheticians, takes such class terms as "tragedy," "comedy," "landscape," "sonata," very seriously. Another example would be Einstein's famous question, "What do we mean by simultaneity at a distance?" This led him to raise the philosophical question, "What is a definition?" And that was bound up with one of those reforms in philosophy which produce revolutions. If Einstein had been content to remain a physicist and not to ask philosophical questions, someone else would have developed the special theory of relativity, or it would not have been developed at all. This is to be sure an oversimplification, but in a short talk of this kind one cannot go into all the complexities of intellectual history.

These two examples lie within the domain of natural science. But no one is only a scientist, and a scientist twenty-four hours a day. No one is anything twenty-four hours a day. One reads books, listens to music, talks with one's friends, unless one is some sort of monster. I think it can be shown that the two questions I have used as my examples came into science from philosophy, and that the first of the two, the question of species, got into philosophy from religion. For there, one species, that of mankind, was dogmatically believed to be a collection of irreducible individuals. But the same question arose in painting and sculpture when the Italian Renaissance actually refused to conform to one set of rules, which is the only justification I have ever found for Burckhardt's theory of what the Renaissance really was. It was given more support from geographical, archeological, and astronomical discoveries in the sixteenth century. And possibly, though here I am far from being sure, it was also stimulated by the various inventions that began to be made at that time. May I interrupt for a moment to say that I am not maintaining that there was a *Zeitgeist* or any other kind of *Geist* expressing itself here, unless one is willing to admit that a *Geist* may be schizophrenic.

Now the greatest source of intellectual dissatisfaction is bound to come from a study of the various arts, history, and philosophy. For such studies are incorrigibly recalcitrant to codification. One no sooner comes up with a beautiful generalization than a new fact bursts in upon one and upsets it. Artistic genera always collapse almost as soon as they

are established. Historical laws are notorious for their habit
of being broken. Metaphysical theories and systems are almost
as ephemeral as the minds that originated them, unless, like
Aristotelianism, they can wear a number of disguises. It is,
of course, always possible to make any law or generalization
seem reasonable by keeping it on a high level of abstraction.
An oyster and a logarithm seem normally to have nothing in
common, but one can always say that at least their names
occurred to me at the same time. The fact has relevance only
to my biography and to the history of President Odegaard's
inauguration. But I doubt that it will loom large in the
history books of the future. We may therefore dismiss such
homogeneity from any further consideration.

My point is that the arts, history, and philosophy are three
fields more distinguished for the heterogeneity of their subject matters than for their unity. If the humanists would
wake up to this fact, they would seize upon it as one of the
cardinal differentiae of human beings. We are, as has been
pointed out by others, historical animals. We are mutable,
and, though it is theoretically possible to explain why the
changes occur when they do occur, that does not eliminate
them. Moreover, it is precisely these fields that enter into
the consciousness of the average citizen, whereas the sciences
remain restricted territory to most of us. If the humanists
would build on this, their teaching would prove more of a
blessing to their students than if they insisted on imitating
the scientists.

Finally, I should like to suggest that some humanists, if
not all, spend a little time studying the humanistic implications of the sciences. This is especially important in an age
like our own when the prestige of science, both pure and

applied, is rightly enough pre-eminent. There is no conflict between, for instance, literary and scientific talent. Lucretius, Dante, Goethe, and, in the nineteenth century, Tennyson and Browning were all interested in the science of their time, and Goethe actually did some scientific work. No one can forget the long discourse of the Angel Raphael to Adam on astronomy that occurs in *Paradise Lost,* a discourse that must have been as moving to the seventeenth-century reader as it was to Adam. Didactic poems have gone out of style, but what about the anthropological passages in *The Waste Land?* How about Zola's genetic theories and their ingression into his novels? How about Hardy's materialism, which certainly must have emerged from what he had read of science? And, if one is willing to call psychology a science, how about the influence of Freud on painting, fiction, and biography? You may say that these scientific items are all obsolete by now— though psychoanalysis still seems to flourish for the greater good of most of us—but that is irrelevant to my point. My point is that some artists and writers have successfully seen the implications of scientific theories for human life and have brought them out in their works.

These four tasks, and there are many others, are neglected by most practitioners of the humanities, and, since they prefer to stick to interests that are no longer those of our civilization, they have had to retreat further and further into their cells until now nobody pays them much attention. The humanities are neither dead nor dying, but it is not the universities on the whole that are keeping them alive. There has never yet been a society, except possibly that of the Bushmen, that has not had its artists and philosophers and, indeed, its historians. To make room for them has been accepted as the most natural thing in the world. If the humanists think that modern society has rejected them, and judging from their weeping and wailing that is what they do think, they might ask whether it is not they who have rejected modern society. But I have spoken long enough, and, if I talked for the rest of my remaining years, I could not exhaust the subject. I hope at any rate that I have made a few suggestions that may prove worthy of thought.

G. H. FORSYTH
Chairman, Department of Fine Arts
University of Michigan

Modern Art
and the Humanities

THERE CAN BE NO doubt that the history of art, including modern art, is one of the humanities. My university's catalogue of courses says so—and who can doubt a university catalogue? In the enumeration of subjects that must be sampled by all candidates for the Bachelor of Arts degree, our courses in art history are grouped under the general heading of "Humanities," along with various others in literature and musicology. There we stand, proudly confronting the neighboring categories of "Natural Science" and "Social Science." Our heading, "The Humanities," is set in type just as bold as theirs, and I suppose we should be pleased by this recognition of our coequal importance.

Actually, such splendid isolation disconcerts me. Like many of my colleagues in the humanities, I do not care to be categorized into a gilded cage of culture. We feel that we should be concerned with the human implications of every subject and that we should, in this human sense, take all

knowledge to be our province including—especially in the
modern world—a knowledge of science. As an architect I
personally am fascinated by technological developments, particularly in the field of structure, and as a medievalist I cannot
forget the words of the French architect who was called in as
consultant during the construction of Milan Cathedral in
1400. To the Italian architects, who were presumably being
a bit arty about the job, he sternly announced that art without science is nothing (*Ars sine scientia nihil est*).

My purpose here today is to stress the importance of mutual
respect and close understanding between the modern humanists and the modern scientists and to suggest that the visual
arts provide a most effective channel of communication between the two. As to mutual respect, it is curious that scientists, who are supposedly narrow specialists, often show
great admiration for our subject and sympathetic understanding of its aims—more, indeed, than we evince toward theirs.
For example, permit me to quote some remarks by Dr. Julius
A. Stratton, chancellor of Massachusetts Institute of Technology, and himself a theoretical physicist. He says:

> The trend toward the theoretical is part and parcel of the
> evolving character of Science and Engineering and we are bound
> to give our students a greater mastery of the tools of analysis.
> What I fear is that in the process we are failing to develop other
> priceless powers of perception. . . . My whole argument rests on
> the conviction that analysis divorced from physical objectivity is
> sterile. Whether the boy learns to draft or to paint or to use a
> machine tool with adequate professional skill seems to me rela-
> tively unimportant. I do want him to gain a sense of the con-
> crete, to have a direct experience with the objects about which
> he thinks.
> It may seem strange to you, coming as it does from a

theoretical physicist, but I think it no more important that an M.I.T. graduate should have mastered the calculus than I do that he should have developed the capacity to see, a sense of form and shape and design, and a feeling for the plasticity of matter.[1]

Dr. Stratton's comments show a remarkable appreciation of the value of art as direct experience of tangible reality. Equally striking are the words of J. Arthur Thomson, a distinguished historian of science, concerning the importance of the humanities in general. He goes so far as to say that "Science is, in a true sense, one of the Humanities."

Not only is the pure scientist apt to maintain this respectful attitude toward art and the humanities, but the engineer and the manufacturer often pay similar tributes. Mr. Arthur A. Houghton, Jr., is president of Steuben Glass, a small firm that produces art glass of the finest design and quality, and he is also vice-president of the parent company, the Corning Glass Works, which is a giant in the mass production field. In a statement of policy published in 1951, he writes:

> Steuben and Corning are different as to problems, products and goals, but to an extraordinary degree we have been able to apply the same principles of design to Steuben's fine crystal and to Corning's multiple mass-market items. What we have done, others can do with equal benefit to their prestige and their profits. . . . In all truth, I can say that we have never once regretted our determination to place so much emphasis on design.[2]

[1] From a letter sent in 1952 by Dr. Julius A. Stratton, chancellor of the Massachusetts Institute of Technology, to the Committee for the Study of the Visual Arts at the Massachusetts Institute of Technology.

[2] Arthur A. Houghton, Jr., *Design Policy within Industry as a Responsibility of High-Level Management* (paper read at an international congress of the Council of Industrial Design, London, 1951; published by Steuben Glass, Inc., 1951), pp. 31-32.

Obviously, then, those of us who are concerned with art and the humanities need not feel on the defensive in the modern world. We have friends, even among the men of science and technology, who understand and respect our field of interest. Such respectful attention should give us confidence to realize an important fact, namely, that the arts have tremendous significance as a channel—perhaps the only channel —through which the rarefied abstractions of modern science can penetrate the world of men, can be humanized. The value of this channel has been well expressed by F. S. C. Northrop, who writes:

> The real as conceived by contemporary science is not even such that it can be grasped by the imagination, to say nothing about it being sensed; only formally by the intellect can it be known. Nevertheless, comprehend it we must. Otherwise our philosophy of the theoretic component and our conduct flowing out of it will be false to the nature of things. . . . What cannot be grasped by everyone literally in terms of the concepts of the scientist and scientific philosopher, can be suggested and presented analogically with vividness and moving power, by recourse to the concepts by intuition of the artist. Here the art of the future will find its new message for men. Its task will be to take the new conception of the theoretic component of reality which contemporary science is now making articulate, and to convey this conception metaphorically, in terms of the vivid aesthetic materials given in immediate intuition. . . . The emotions, not merely of the masses, but of all of us, and especially all humanists, are still geared to the old conceptions. . . . Our emotions, still correlated with an outmoded doctrine, have yet to be reconstructed in terms of the new intellectual outlook. . . . Such is the difficulty, and by the same measure the importance, of the task of the artist of the future.[3]

[3] F. S. C. Northrop, The Logic of the Sciences and the Humanities (New York: Macmillan Co., 1949), pp. 184-87.

Northrop is speaking of poetry as well as visual art, and he does not demonstrate his meaning by specific examples from either field. In my remaining time, I shall attempt to illustrate his thought by examples from my own field of the visual arts; for I believe that modern painting, sculpture, and architecture have had considerable success already in suggesting "with vividness and moving power" some of the basic conceptions of modern science. I shall limit myself to that one which has most popular appeal, namely, the modern scientific concept of space. Even before the sputniks made us all crane our necks upward, the possibility of space travel had caught the imagination of the public, as evidenced by science fiction and "comics." The vast reaches of the universe are now in the public domain.

The easiest way to demonstrate modern spatial concepts in art is to show them developing out of—and away from—earlier ones. Much of the great art of the world has indicated no interest whatever in space. The Byzantine mosaic in Figure 1 is as flat and airless as a playing card. For our purposes, however, we can begin with the ideas about space that were formulated in artistic practice during the Italian Renaissance. In the fifteenth century, Italian painters established a new theory of art. This theory, which may seem obvious and trivial, has been described by a modern commentator, Dr. Erwin Panofsky, as being "the most problematic dogma of aesthetic theory: the dogma that a work of art is the direct and faithful representation of a natural object." [4] A Renaissance picture, for example, was conceived as a "window through which we

---

[4] Erwin Panofsky, *The Codex Huygens and Leonardo da Vinci's Art Theory* (London: Warburg Institute, 1940), p. 90.

look out into a section of the visible world," in the words of Alberti. He was an early expounder of the idea and was one of the first Renaissance theorists to develop a geometric system for creating on a flat surface such an illusion of a window opening out upon visible reality. The geometric system was, of course, linear perspective, the greatest and, indeed, the key invention of Renaissance art.

It is highly significant that a modern audience understands immediately what is meant by this five-hundred-year-old theory. Linear perspective is still our normal way of thinking about space. As everyone knows, it is a simple method of "capturing" on a flat surface a certain portion of space and its contents. A woodcut by Dürer (Fig. 2) provides an excellent illustration. It is from his *Treatise on Descriptive Geometry*, published in 1525. The woodcut is valuable not only as showing how the perspective system works, but also as revealing its great limitation, that it is a fixed, or absolute, system. It is fixed in space, because the artist's eye must look only through a peephole held in place by a setscrew and also because the sitter and his surroundings must retain their present positions relative to each other and to the artist's eye. It is fixed in time, because there is no way to represent on the same projection the situation at some subsequent moment when the artist or his subject may have changed their relative positions. Finally, the system is based on a fixed concept of matter, because, while the painter is working, the objects in the picture must retain their integrity as solids, clearly defined and unchanging in outer appearance.

The absoluteness of the system is even more evident in a diagram (Fig. 3) from a modern manual on drawing. The book lying on the table may be projected onto the glass plate only if the draftsman keeps his chin on the pile of books and if the book on the table is not moved. Time holds its breath so that spatial relations may not change. And, of course, while the draftsman is at work, the book itself must be let alone. If anyone disturbs its outer integrity as a material object, for instance by turning the pages to see what is inside, the perspective system collapses.

Granting that these three absolutes of time, space, and matter are not tampered with, the book on the table can be projected onto the glass plate successfully, either in a head-on view, so that its sides appear to converge toward a single vanishing point, or in a diagonal view, so that they appear to converge toward two vanishing points (Fig. 4). In either case, a vanishing point terminates an axis of convergence. In the upper view, a single such axis extends to the horizon directly ahead of us. In the lower one, two such axes branch off to left and right.

Turning now from the method and implications of linear perspective to actual results, we can watch the new system take effect in early Renaissance painting. In a picture (Fig. 5) by Duccio, which was painted in the fourteenth century and antecedes Alberti and the other creators of perspective theory by a hundred years, we still see the old medieval casualness about arranging forms in space. Here, on a photograph of the painting, the lines of the architecture have been carried out to their intersection. They intersect at a number of points, quite at random, and not at a single point on the horizon, as required by perspective theory. In a picture (Fig. 6) by the fifteenth-century painter Masolino, who was a contemporary of Alberti, the architectural lines do conform to the new theory. They converge correctly toward a single vanishing

point and define an axis of convergence, which is the axis of
the street that opens before us. The medieval casualness and
rambling character are gone. Instead, the observer finds himself in the firm grip of an inelastic geometric system. As in the
diagram shown earlier, his chin is, so to speak, resting on a
pile of books.

Once firmly established, the Renaissance system of linear
perspective stood unchallenged almost down to our own day.
For most people, it is still unchallenged and no more to be
questioned than a picture made by the perspective machine
we call a camera.

By the seventeenth century, the absolute concept of space
that underlies linear perspective had come fully into its own,
attended by other absolutist concepts of awesome proportions.
The gardens of Versailles, laid out by Le Nôtre in about 1670,
provide a perfect example (Fig. 7). In this case, it is not a
picture but Nature herself that is subjected to the laws of
Renaissance perspective. An axis of convergence is opened,
quite literally, to the horizon before us, and others branch
out to left and right. As the fixed observer of this space system, corresponding to the man shown in our earlier slide with
his chin on a pile of books, we must imagine Louis XIV seated
amid his court on the nearby terrace, whence he liked to
watch the sun set at the far end of the great axis before him.
The geometric system of his garden, as rigid as the sun's orbit,
was a fitting parallel to the equally rigid organization of his
realm. Its axes—political, social, economic, and educational—
also radiated outward from him, the fixed point of reference.

Religious art of the seventeenth century conformed to the
same principles, and astonishing perspectives were opened
into the heavenly realm. The ceiling of the Church of Sant'

Ignazio in Rome is actually a curving surface, not much higher than the six windows visible in our illustration (Fig. 8). Yet the painter, Pozzo, has contrived to project onto this curved plane a perspective of imaginary columns whose converging lines carry the eye up into space eternal. The scene is filled with spiraling clouds and figures, and such rhythmic movement of masses through space is reminiscent of the principles of celestial mechanics developed by Newton in the same period. Yet the underlying concept of space, like Newton's, is just as absolute as the garden of Versailles. The proof is that Pozzo has been careful to set an inscription in the center of the floor, advising the observer to view the ceiling from that point only. Seen from anywhere else, the whole perspective structure appears to topple.

Coming down to the mid-nineteenth century, we find the same concepts predominant. When Baron Haussmann, the vigorous city planner of Napoleon III, undertook to modernize the plan of Paris, he did so by cutting great boulevards through the city (Fig. 9). These *rues corridors,* as they are appropriately called, formed great perspective axes, radiating out from nodal points in the huge plan. No doubt, Louis XIV would have understood them perfectly and would have applauded.

Yet, it is in this same nineteenth century that a new attitude toward perspective and, implicitly, toward space, makes its appearance. In the paintings of Cézanne, a new departure is evident. For example, he has painted the still life reproduced in Figure 10 not from one point of view but from several different ones. He shows the left-hand jar as seen directly from the side, but he also gives us a plunging view down into its interior, and he has not hesitated to "bend down" the left-hand side of the table more than the right, as if the left side were seen more from above. After fifty years of modern art, we are not scandalized by such minor disruptions of Renaissance perspective. But in 1885, when this picture was painted, the concept of the single viewpoint in a picture was so entrenched that outraged old ladies attacked Cézanne's pictures with umbrellas, and kinder souls said the poor man had defective eyesight.

Much ruder shocks were in store for the public. In about 1908 two young painters in Paris, Picasso and Braque, undertook to carry Cézanne's experiments further. The result was the Cubist movement. The name, based on a chance remark by Matisse, is rather unfortunate. In an early Cubist painting such as the one shown in Figure 11—"The Reservoir," by Picasso, 1909—the main thing is not the simplified cubes but the new implications as to space. The perspective lines go in all directions. They are more divergent than those in the early fourteenth-century painting we saw and would probably give a Renaissance art theorist convulsions. The reason is that Picasso has not stood outside the picture space and made a snapshot of it, taken from one point of view and at one instant of time. Instead, he has stepped into his picture space and has recorded its contents from a number of different positions. The old absolute fixity of space, as seen from a single viewpoint, has broken down. So has the absolute fixity of time, because the picture is not the record of a single instant. It records, rather, a whole sequence of observations, and therefore time is one of its dimensions. In this picture, we have an esthetic equivalent of space-time.

The third absolute, that of material substance, is still intact. The cubes are quite substantial. Even here, however, there is a suggestion of things to come. The surfaces of the

Fig. 1. Madonna and Child between Emperor John II and Empress Irene. Istanbul, Hagia Sophia. Photo courtesy of the Byzantine Institute

Fig. 2. Albrecht Dürer. Drawing technique. Woodcut, 1525. Photo from *Dürer*, Librairie Hachette, Paris

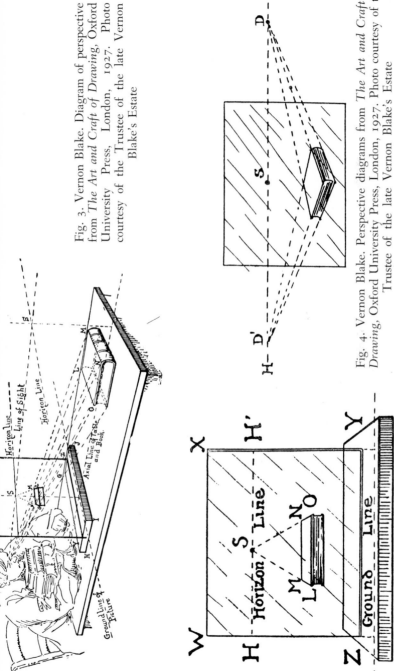

Fig. 3. Vernon Blake. Diagram of perspective from *The Art and Craft of Drawing*, Oxford University Press, London, 1927. Photo courtesy of the Trustee of the late Vernon Blake's Estate

Fig. 4. Vernon Blake. Perspective diagrams from *The Art and Craft of Drawing*, Oxford University Press, London, 1927. Photo courtesy of the Trustee of the late Vernon Blake's Estate

Fig. 5. Duccio. Christ's Sermon to the Apostles. Siena, Opera del Duomo. Perspective analysis by Ransom R. Patrick

Fig. 6. Masolino. The Feast of Herod. Baptistery, Castiglione d'Olona. Alinari Photo

Fig. 7. Garden axis, Versailles. Photo from *Jardins de France* by P. Péan, A. Vincent, Paris, 1925

Fig. 8. Andrea Pozzo. Glorification of St. Ignatius. Rome, S. Ignazio. Alinari Photo

Fig. 9. Avenue de l'Opéra, Paris. Photo from *Space, Time and Architecture*
by Siegfried Giedion, Harvard University Press, 1954

Fig. 10. Paul Cézanne. Nature Morte à la Commode, 1883-87. Fogg Art Museum. Photo courtesy of the Fogg Art Museum, Harvard University, Maurice Wertheim Collection

Fig. 11. Pablo Picasso. Le Réservoir, Horta de Ebro, 1909. Paris, Private
Collection

Fig. 12. Pablo Picasso. L'Arlésienne, 1911-12. Walter P. Chrysler, Jr., Collection

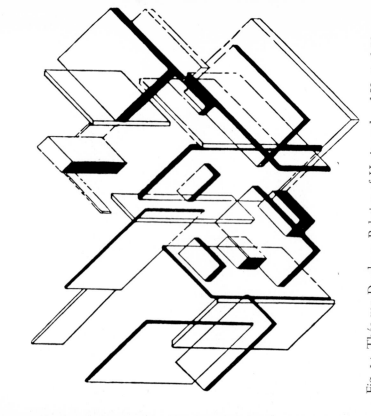

Fig. 14. Théo van Doesburg. Relation of Horizontal and Vertical Planes. Photo from *Space, Time and Architecture* by Siegfried Giedion, Harvard University Press, 1954

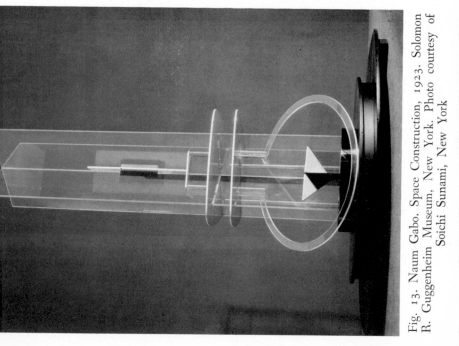

Fig. 13. Naum Gabo. Space Construction, 1923. Solomon R. Guggenheim Museum, New York. Photo courtesy of Soichi Sunami, New York

Fig. 15. Richard Neutra. The Lovell House, Los Angeles. Photo courtesy of Richard Neutra

Fig. 16. Frank Lloyd Wright. Falling Water, Bear Run, Pennsylvania. Photo by Bill Hedrich, Hedrich-Blessing

Fig. 17. Frank Lloyd Wright. Falling Water, Bear Run, Pennsylvania. Photo by Bill Hedrich, Hedrich-Blessing

Fig. 18. Frank Lloyd Wright. Falling Water, Bear Run, Pennsylvania. Photo by Bill Hedrich, Hedrich-Blessing

Fig. 19. "The Pretzel" Traffic Interchange, Kew Gardens, New York, as it appeared in 1947. Photo from *Space, Time and Architecture* by Siegfried Giedion, Harvard University Press, 1954

cubes are very emphatically defined as planes. Most of them are sharply outlined and isolated, and many of them are graded violently from light to dark, as if a light had flashed across their sheer surfaces. One feels it would be easy to disassemble the cubes into their constituent planes, like dismounting the flats of a stage set. This is precisely the next step the Cubists took.

In Picasso's sketch (Fig. 12) called "Woman of Arles," made in 1911 or 1912, the step has been taken, and matter itself has lost its old impenetrability and absolute distinction from space. The figure has no definite outline but fuses into space—is, indeed, merely a locus of energies or a condensation of space itself. The interpenetrating lines, planes, textures, and shadings form a crystalline, translucent, almost disembodied image that is yet pulsating with enormous energy. It is like tossing into the air a deck of cards or, better yet, sheets of transparent plastic. It is as if one suddenly riffled through the pages of the book that lay on the table in our diagram of Renaissance perspective. Moreover, the multiple points of view and the time dimension are present, as shown by the fact that the woman's head is seen in full face and in double profile, as if it rotated and nodded before our eyes.

Since descriptive detail is kept to a minimum and the forms are reduced to diagrammatic simplicity, the picture has an abstractness like that of a scientific diagram. Such a resemblance is entirely appropriate; for similar developments were occurring at the same time in science. In that field, also, old certitudes were being displaced by profounder, more dynamic, more closely knit concepts of space, time, and matter. It is a most remarkable fact that an artist like Picasso, who could not possibly understand the mathematical statement of

the four-dimensional space-time continuum and who probably
had never heard of Einstein in 1912, could nevertheless arrive at a parallel statement in the esthetic terms appropriate to
painting. We have here a resounding example of the type of
art Northrop demands of the modern artist—an art that can
convey metaphorically in terms of vivid esthetic materials the
new scientific concepts and that can thereby help to recon-
struct men's emotions in terms of the new intellectual outlook.

Not only painting, but also sculpture began to reflect the
new concepts. In the so-called "Space Construction" (Fig. 13)
by the Russian, Naum Gabo, the interpenetrating planes and
lines have the same implications of space and energy as the
painting by Picasso. The planes, being of transparent material,
convey a similar effect of disembodied form, of penetrability.
Moreover, their transparency, combined with the fact that
they are also reflecting surfaces, like mirrors, produces an im-
pression of multiple images and of many viewpoints that is
quite comparable to the space-time effect of the painting. One
experiences such a structure from all sides, and through and
through, and feels almost compelled to walk around it. Quite
appropriately, sculpture of this kind has been described as a
"space modulator."

Its total abstraction, without any resemblance to natural
forms, appears in a sketch made in about 1920 (Fig. 14).
The artist, a Dutchman named Van Doesburg, called it simply
"Relation of Horizontal and Vertical Planes." Here is another
"space modulator," in terms of a drawing this time, but one's
first reaction is probably that it represents a building. Actually,
it was meant simply as an exercise, like a musical étude. The
implications for architecture are obvious, however, and ar-

chitects adopted the new spatial concepts when clients were ready to accept them and as soon as the cumbrous building industry was prepared to implement them economically.

In 1929 Neutra built the Lovell house in Los Angeles (Fig. 15). The relation between a structure of this type and Van Doesburg's sketch is manifest. It is composed not from any single viewpoint but from many and offers the observer a multiple experience of space, over and under, inside and outside, through and through. The old massiveness of architecture is gone. No longer is the building thought of as an opaque box consisting of the traditional four walls and a roof. It is a "space modulator" to be lived in.

A later and more famous example of the same type is the Kaufman house at Bear Run, Pennsylvania (Fig. 16). It was built in 1936 by Frank Lloyd Wright. Such a design shatters completely the old Renaissance absolutes of space, time, and matter. It is a total experience of all three at once. A sheaf of planes hovers in a continuous space that we experience progressively. The space is experienced through time, and there is no sharp demarcation between mass and void. When we are inside the house, our attention is drawn toward the outside, and vice versa (Fig. 17).

Esthetically, this is a culmination of the experiments begun by Cézanne and carried forward by Picasso. To my mind, it is another example satisfying perfectly Northrop's demand for a modern art that can help to adjust men's emotions to the new scientific concepts of the world. Inevitably, I believe, any perceptive person living in such a house would feel a harmony between nature as we experience it and nature as we know it to be (Fig. 18). The woodland scene is combined happily with the hovering planes of the architecture, and the occupant can feel at home in both. He can accept our fearful new cosmos.

An objection may be raised that only a few people can live in, or even see, such a house and that modern paintings and sculpture are sequestered in museums and private collections where a small minority of the public ever looks at them and even fewer understand them. No doubt this is true. Nevertheless, art—even the most advanced, experimental art—has a curious way of seeping out into the main currents of life and giving a new color to the opinions and preferences of the public. This is especially true in our period, when the latest productions of artists and architects are circulated through the mass media of communication. The grid patterns of Mondrian, a severely abstract modern painter, are commonplace ornaments for floor linoleum; and the whimsical forms tossed off by the French painter, Arp, have invaded the furniture industry and have produced the so-called "Arp form," or "kidney" pattern for tables. In the case of architecture, the chain reaction of influences is equally clear. Every architect in the country, and a vast number of laymen, must be perfectly familiar through photographs and articles with the Kaufman house and with other experiments by the architectural pioneers of our time. The proof is that designers of a large proportion of the ordinary buildings being erected around us, such as modest suburban homes, shopping centers, and the like, attempt to follow the lead of the pioneers and to strike out further on their own. Some do so with amazing success.

My final example is a complex junction of highways near New York City, which has been nicknamed "The Pretzel" (Fig. 19). With this view in mind, I should like to return to the idea I began with, namely, the present-day need for a broad definition of the humanities. We have been considering the value of art as an aid in the adjustment of men's emotions to new scientific concepts instead of older, outmoded ideas of absolute time, space, and matter. An expressway such as this, whipping freely across the open countryside, is a vivid metaphor of the space-time continuum. The traveler is liberated from any fixed viewpoint, since he himself is a rapidly moving point. With perceptions heightened by speed, he can experience space unfolding in time and time recorded in space, so that they are two aspects of the same thing, space-time.

Yet the expressway, which can convey this modern sensation with such vividness and immediacy, is not a work of art in the usual sense and certainly does not reflect esthetic experiments by any artist or architect. Must it, therefore, be considered outside the field of interest of modern art and, consequently, of the humanities? I hardly think so. We regard the great aqueducts as among the noblest achievements of Roman architecture, and future historians will probably appraise our highway systems in much the same way. Utility does not defile a work of art.

In my opinion, a technological tour de force such as this is a masterpiece of modern art, in the broad sense of that term, and is bound to interest any truly modern humanist. He knows that a successful adjustment between man's emotional responses and the new world of science is desperately important, and he values art, whether pure or applied, as an aid in this adjustment, as a valuable ally of the humanities.

INAUGURAL ADDRESSES

NATHAN M. PUSEY
President, Harvard University

The Joint Responsibility
of Public and Private Universities

I SHOULD LIKE to talk today about American private and public institutions of higher education. I shall proceed first briefly to review the development of these differing approaches to a common goal and then make a short comment about the nature of the enormous responsibilities that now confront the two kinds of institutions jointly.

I am moved to this undertaking because of an assumption one is forever encountering that public and private institutions are somehow, or should be, engaged in deadly combat. Partisans on the one side, for example, are not above trying to establish the idea that state universities are godless, socialistic institutions for promoting statism; or, on the other hand, that private universities are undemocratic citadels of aristocratic privilege. Such statements seem to me to be invidious nonsense. Nor do I find more acceptable claims that state institutions are the only ones concerned to provide educational opportunities for the poor and ambitious, or that private institutions are alone suited to furnish the kind of education required for the exceptionally able. My qualifications for entering what is widely recognized to be a dangerous area of debate may be strongly compounded of innocence, but at least they are also well seasoned with good will. In any event I speak as the president of a university that was for two hundred years partly supported by public funds, although it is now largely private.

State universities are older than is commonly thought. Twenty-one of them were founded before the Civil War, beginning with Georgia in 1785 and North Carolina in 1789. Thus, if length of residence among us is an indication of American character, surely these institutions are as "American" as any. When one recalls that there were only nine institutions of higher learning established in colonial America, it is also clear that a number of the public institutions have as much claim to the dignity and respect of age as do most of the private ones.

At the outset all of the state universities had to struggle against indifference—and frequently, too, against active hostility—to get themselves established. They had to keep on struggling to survive. The beginnings of none of them, no more than the beginnings of most of the private ones, were especially impressive. For example, we are told that, in its early years, the University of North Carolina had a twenty-four-year-old president and a faculty of three, consisting of "a French ex-monk, a deserter from the British Navy, and a strolling player." [1] It would be interesting to know what subjects each of them taught. Perhaps you will not mind, in view

[1] George P. Schmidt, *The Old Time College President* (New York: Columbia University Press, 1930), p. 87.

of your university's present eminence, if I suggest as a further example that there was a degree of quixotism in giving the name "university" to the territorial institution first established here in 1861.

But in time the state universities came of age. There are several markers to indicate steps along the way. One was the opening of the University of Virginia in 1825. Another was the work of Henry P. Tappan at Michigan in the 1850's. A third was the passage of the Morrill Act in 1862, which enabled several of the state universities, by keeping the land grants in their own hands, for the first time substantially to strengthen themselves. Perhaps for most the time of majority was to come still later. In any event, nowhere before the Civil War did state legislatures provide serious or steady support for their universities.[2] But today there are many state universities, the majority of them strong and large. Together they carry a considerable part of the total burden of higher education in America. I suspect even the most partisan supporter of private institutions, if he has actually looked at the other kind recently, will have to agree that in all likelihood they are here to stay.

A point apparently imperfectly understood about state universities is that they were not imposed upon our country by a special interest group, but rather grew in response to valid educational needs. Though it is of course obvious that these institutions were intended to provide more educational opportunity, it is an oversimplification to say that their primary purpose was to make it possible for poor boys to go

[2] Richard Hofstadter and C. DeWitt Hardy, *The Development and Scope of Higher Education in the United States* (New York: Columbia University Press, 1952), pp. 28, 44.

to college. Indeed, the many small, privately supported, denominational colleges that everywhere predated the state universities were perhaps better designed, because of their low costs and wide dispersion, to fill this role. As a matter of fact it was not uncommon in the early years of the state universities to find the partisans of the private colleges hurling the nasty epithet "aristocratic" at state universities because they did not in the beginning offer free tuition and often were more attractive to the sons of the wealthy than were the small colleges.[3] It is impossible not to conclude that from the beginning both kinds of institutions could and did under varying circumstances offer educational opportunity to both pecunious and impecunious students, just as they do today.

There were other, deeper reasons that stimulated the birth of state universities. One was the justified complaint that the curriculum of the small denominational college was narrow and excessively "literary" because it was rooted solely in Greek, Latin, and mathematics—in keeping with an academic tradition designed centuries before to meet the needs of young men most of whom were preparing for the ministry or for teaching. It is not fair completely to condemn this course of study because, like programs of liberal education in any age, it simply eschewed vocational concern to concentrate on helping individuals, by cultivating their minds and widening their interests, to live wisely, happily, and well. This early curriculum had, and has, its merits. But as the country grew, and economic interests and professions multiplied, it became increasingly difficult to maintain that it was, and should always

[3] Richard Hofstadter and Walter P. Metzger, *The Development of Academic Freedom in the United States* (New York: Columbia University Press, 1955), p. 246.

be, the *only* curriculum. And, since there was almost no disposition within the early college to alter or widen it, a movement for a new kind of institution, less bound by tradition, understandably got under way.

The small denominational college was also thought to be inadequate because of its religious particularity. Founded by and intended to serve the interests of special groups, these institutions all too frequently permitted questions of church membership to weigh too heavily in what were primarily educational concerns, and they never succeeded in throwing off the suspicion of partiality. Again it is not surprising that many felt a need for a new kind of higher learning, which would belong, as it was said, to "all the people," above, or outside, sectarian control. Incidentally, this should not be understood to imply, as their self-regarding opponents were even then not above asserting, that the desired publicly supported institutions set out deliberately to be "godless."

Still another shortcoming of the older privately supported institutions of higher learning that helped forward the movement for state universities was faculty resistance to change. Fierce and suspicious faculty opposition often greeted the ambitious efforts of enlightened presidents and teachers to turn these colleges into universities—to make them communities not of pedagogues giving elementary instruction, but of mature scholars. In a very real sense the movement for state universities was thus only part of a larger movement in the United States to establish here institutions of truly higher learning, built after Continental models, which because of their advanced scholarship would really deserve the name of "university." Incidentally, we are again in a period in which this proud name is being bestowed rather lightly, at times, it would seem, almost barbarically. But, however that may be, much of the leadership in this effort which produced true universities among us for the first time came from private institutions. The strongest of them, together with new private institutions such as Hopkins, and later Chicago, succeeded as well as any in growing to meet the new standard. Indeed, they led the way. But they were flanked by a number of public institutions, originally little better than colleges, which, beginning in the seventies and eighties of the last century, succeeded in transforming themselves into true universities.

Thus, the state university movement, appealing to a wider range of interest and concern, and calling for a wider curriculum, for increased emphasis on science, and for more and more research, was a movement for a new kind of institution in our land whose distinction would be as much in the quality of its advanced scholarship as in the reach of its quantitative appeal.

Still a further and utterly practical reason why many individuals thought the private institutions could not by themselves furnish the higher education our nation required was their weak financial backing. Before the Civil War there were 516 colleges established in the 16 states of the union. Of this number only 104 survived. One has only to look back a short time to Principal Mercer's frontier "university" in the days before Washington's statehood to grasp how great was the difference between the vision and the realization in the founding era of state universities. As a contemporary observer said, "[Colleges] are duly lauded and puffed for a day; and then they sink to be heard of no more." [4]

Early advocates of state-supported institutions were ap-

[4] *Ibid.*, pp. 211-12.

palled by the proliferation of small sectarian colleges and shocked by the constricted financial limitations within which virtually all of them had to struggle. The achievement of strong education, it seemed to them, called for concentration of resources, and they were fully persuaded that higher education was of such importance to the people that a state must adequately support it. Only after these institutions won consistent financial support—as did Michigan and Wisconsin among early examples—did they grow strong in state after state and contribute to the impressive, if perhaps still inadequate, network of substantial institutions we have today.

It seems almost superfluous to say that ample and consistent financing is essential for all educational institutions with convictions of excellence. There have been some private institutions that have demonstrated ability to get such support without benefit of tax income, or with only very meager help from this source; but it has also been clearly demonstrated that an adequate share of tax income is a powerful encouragement to the development of strong, publicly supported institutions of higher learning. It is to be hoped, therefore, that both kinds of support, now inextricably mixed, will continue and increase, and that the two kinds of institutions, both provided with ample resources, will continue to advance.

Thus far my argument has led me to concentrate attention on their similarities, but there are also significant points of difference between public and private institutions. Among these are differences in tradition, concerning the percentage of their income derived from different sources, the range of their responsibilities, their educational emphases, the kinds of pressures that play upon them, above all their forms of control. And these are important. We in the private institutions

believe strongly that it is essential for the health of the whole
of higher education in America that there always be strong
private colleges and universities kept safely beyond the reach
of political control. We recognize that the best of the relatively
small private colleges are as successful as any institutions in
the pursuit of excellence. We do not agree, however, that
only small colleges are concerned for their students as individuals. But we feel it is especially important for the health
of our total educational enterprise that large private universities which have acquired extraordinary educational resources, and which have served the highest educational standards over a long period of time, continue strong and independent. By concentrating their attention, or, perhaps it is
fair to say, by neglecting obligations that a state university
cannot neglect, they have a special capacity sometimes to
move more quickly in pursuit of new interests and can work
more consistently and more single-mindedly to advance standards. These capacities are important for the whole of higher
education. But we know, too, that in the past private institutions have many times been helped to awareness of new
responsibility and pushed from narrowness, complacency, and
conservatism by the competition of state universities; and we
suspect (and hope) this may also be true again and again. Nor
should anything I have said here be understood to imply that
the highest standards of academic performance cannot also
be served, even at the most creative levels, in public institutions.

Some years ago a Harvard report on general education spoke
of Jeffersonian and Jacksonian emphases within our educational practice, "the one valuing opportunity as the nurse of

excellence, the other as the guard of equity." [5] It is easy to assert that at the level of higher education one of these functions belongs to one kind of institution, the other to the other, but to do so is to ignore the facts. There are strong public institutions pursuing the highest standards of academic excellence along with strong private ones, and there are many in both groups that fall below—some far below—such standards. One can say the same thing about large or small institutions of higher learning. Some small ones are strong and some are weak, some large ones are weak and some are strong. Neither pretensions nor stereotypes fit the facts. After centuries of development about all we can say is that there are a great many sorts of differences within differing types of educational institutions. It is perhaps time, therefore, that we abandon unwarranted, broad generalizations and learn instead to look at each institution for what it is in itself.

I come now at long last to the main point of my concern today—the heavy responsibility confronting our publicly and our privately supported universities jointly.

We have been told again and again that we shall need in a relatively short time to provide for at least twice as many students as we have acquired the capacity to care for during more than three hundred years of effort. This is true. We shall also need the added resources to make this possible. And we shall have to meet tightening demands for an enormous range of technical and professional training, and, while doing so, and seeking to meet the other legitimate utilitarian ex-

[5] *General Education in a Free Society,* Report of the Harvard Committee, with an introduction by James Bryant Conant (Cambridge, Mass.: Harvard University Press, 1945), p. 34.

pectations confronting our universities at every turn, we shall have to fight to strengthen liberal learning and to extend its influence in every part of our endeavor. We must also, in the national interest, carry more exceptionally talented, ambitious, and dedicated individuals to higher peaks of learning and intellectual interest in many more areas of knowledge than our fathers or grandfathers ever dreamed of. Indeed, in view of our present situation in the world, it would be almost treasonable now to say simply that we need more educational opportunity for more individuals in terms of what we might call "ordinary" post-high-school education; for at the same time we also need more opportunity for able and willing students to go forward to the most difficult, most advanced, most demanding, and most creative kinds of learning—to levels that require extraordinary ability, prolonged concentration of effort, and indomitable ambition. To dismiss or neglect this part of our responsibility with the smear word that its pursuance somehow implies the formation of an "elite" seems to me vicious demagoguery. At the same time the contrary notion that institutions that profess to be devoted to the pursuit of quality have no share in the quantitative aspect of our problem seems to me equally misguided and unrealistic.

It was fortunate for the nation that, in the period between the Civil War and World War I, during the period, that is, when our country as we know it today was coming of age, there were numerous leaders in higher education who, despite occasional differences and varying approaches, labored to adapt to American conditions and traditions the vision of the European university with its emphases upon quality of research and teaching and upon excellence of professional training. Some of the great universities that resulted were private; others, public. The roster of names of the builders of these institutions includes men like Tappan of Michigan, White of Cornell, Folwell of Minnesota, Gilman of California and Johns Hopkins, Van Hise of Wisconsin, Angell of Yale, Harper of Chicago, and Eliot of Harvard. They were the heroes and champions of a truly higher education for America, and it is to them above all that we owe thanks that we now have a widespread public-private university system adequate, we hope, to cope with the enormously more complicated problems of our age.

Our public and our private institutions, created through a variety of circumstances over a long period of time, are now inescapably involved in joint responsibility. If they are competing, it is the friendly competition of two workers on one project. Inseparable considerations of quality and quantity touch education at every point; both make valid claims on every institution. It is therefore necessary for each institution within both groups to do what it can honestly and intelligently to make a contribution to the solution of both aspects of our problem. Surely, in view of its immensity and urgency we can do better now than to waste time in misrepresentation, or in injurious, disputatious hostility among ourselves.

There are a number of things we can do together. We can cooperate within states and in the nation to help governments establish sound educational policies. We can work to prevent duplication of effort in research, in teaching, and in the preservation of books, documents, and other collections that are the tools of teaching and research. We can work together to extend opportunity, to open education to more and more who are qualified, and to provide higher and higher education to the highly able who can be encouraged to pursue it. Above all we can work together to create better general understanding of the nature and need for higher education, and to obtain more generous support for it.

To me our most pressing present problem is to promote this kind of understanding. At the very beginning of the movement to establish state universities, forces within the world of higher education working against qualitative achievements were given new strength. The movement to widen educational opportunity brought with it, in Professor Hofstadter's words, a certain "disdain for authority and excellence and *expertise* of all kinds." [6] Mr. Hofstadter appropriately quotes President Francis Wayland of Brown, who said at the very outset of the university movement in America that "the old practice of assigning academic rank at commencement had often been 'dropped like a polluted thing' because administrators were 'awed by the hoarse growl of popular discontent.' " As early as 1855 the president of the University of Georgia remarked that the American people were "generally satisfied with the *name* of a college, and sought for their sons not so much an education as a degree." [7]

There is, indeed, much for all in higher education to do if at this moment of our history we are to give America's young people not the name, but the *experience* of higher education and give the nation the kinds of educated individuals she now so seriously needs. So may I say in conclusion it is my sincere hope that we in the private institutions shall stand shoulder to shoulder with you in the publicly supported institutions

[6] Hofstadter and Metzger, *The Development of Academic Freedom in the United States*, p. 245.

[7] *Ibid.*, p. 224.

and together face hopefully and determinedly the grave responsibility before us both.

Some of our universities, public and private, have a particularly deep concern and a large share of responsibility for the upper reaches and more demanding kinds of higher education. Such, I take it, is the position of the University of Washington in this region. It seems to many of us on the outside that you have in your new president a man peculiarly well qualified to lead in discharging this mission.

Charles Odegaard has had a long and varied experience in higher education. A graduate of two private institutions— Dartmouth and Harvard—his subsequent professional activity has been largely in the service of three state universities, Illinois, Michigan, and now Washington. Everywhere he has worked effectively to promote high standards. As professor of history at the University of Illinois, as the executive head of the American Council of Learned Societies, as dean of the School of Literature, Science and the Arts at the University of Michigan, he has shown effective concern for the best interests of higher education. During my term as president of Lawrence College more than half a dozen years ago, I had the privilege, in behalf of its faculty and trustees, of conferring on Charles Odegaard his first honorary degree. More recently I have had the opportunity to observe the extraordinary skill, discrimination, and persuasiveness he has shown in recruiting in Cambridge, Massachusetts, outstanding individuals for the faculty of the University of Michigan. Those of us who have known him and his work have no hesitation in saying that you are to be congratulated on having secured his services for the University of Washington. Especially I should like to say to the members of the faculty that you have found a leader who has always shown himself, in all his administrative posts, to be a "faculty man," one who knows what a university should be at its best, and one who, you may be confident, will work with you to bring this university closer to the image of your heart's best desire.

All of us in higher education face together an enormously complex, difficult, costly, and responsible task. Those of us who have looked on from the outside, from both public and private institutions, feel that those here responsible for the choice of the new leader of the University of Washington have chosen wisely, in imaginative awareness of the quickened seriousness and urgency of our common responsibility. We congratulate them and you, and wish for you and your president a creative mutual relationship, much happiness, and abundant success in furtherance of that high endeavor to which we all are called.

CHARLES E. ODEGAARD
President, University of Washington

Inaugural Address

M<small>R. SHEFELMAN</small> and members of the Board of Regents, Your Excellency Governor Rosellini, honorable members of the Legislature, delegates of sister institutions and of learned and scientific societies, distinguished guests, Dr. Schmitz, faculty, students, alumni, and friends of the University of Washington:

It is an honor for the University of Washington to have President Pusey of Harvard University participate in these inaugural ceremonies by delivering this fine and thoughtful installation address. It is a source of great pleasure to me that he is present on this platform on a day that has very special personal meaning for me. I am reminded of the first time I saw Dr. Pusey after he had assumed the presidency of Harvard University. It was six months or so later that I visited him in Cambridge. After chatting in his office in old Massachusetts Hall, Dr. Pusey walked me down a short corridor to a smallish room, gracefully furnished in eighteenth-century style. A fine portrait of Benjamin Franklin looked wisely and beneficently down on the principal piece of furniture in the room, an oval mahogany table surrounded by eight chairs. Doctor Pusey informed me that this was the meeting room of the Harvard Corporation, which consists of the president, the treasurer, and the five Fellows of Harvard University. He said that he had encountered remarkable devotion in the eminent men of affairs who leave their regular pursuits to meet every other Monday in this room to consider with him the welfare and government of Harvard University. He had found that in the estimation of such men there was no honor or public service in their part of the country that could be offered or obtained that could equal the prestigious invitation to become a member of the Harvard Corporation; for this is, he said, the board room of the oldest corporation in continuous existence in the territory of the United States. Dr. Pusey added, characteristically, it is a very humbling thing to inherit the responsibilities of president of the university.

Indeed, one should stand in awe of universities; great and powerful men, kings and princes, popes and peers, presidents and governors, most in wisdom but some in fear, have held a decent respect for the influence—the ultimate leadership—that universities have exerted over the past eight hundred years. There must be something special about universities for them to have this extraordinary survival power, for them to retain their identity and continuity over all these centuries of conflict and change in Europe; to be carried forth to blossom in the new world from the rocky shores of New England to these forested hills of Puget Sound; or to be injected as foreign imports from the West into the colonial territories of Asia and Africa only to survive the demise of the imperial authority as those former colonies have become sovereign powers.

Social inventions have come and gone over the centuries. Few have had the resiliency of this medieval invention, the university. For over eight hundred years universities have had their ups and downs, only to emerge after each languishment more vigorous and influential than before.

What, then, is this durable thing, a university? This question has been asked many times before, especially, and appropriately so, on occasions such as this. The most frequent answer, I suppose, has been "a community of scholars." Good words, meaningful words, repeated often, sometimes slip into triteness, lose their savor, and are shrugged off with a kind of bored indifference. These words, this phrase, "community of scholars," actually had a rich significance in the very beginning of universities, and it has continuing relevance in our own day. It still warrants our attention.

There were scholars, of course, well before the Middle Ages. The word itself is of Latin origin and goes back to the Romans. The force of the phrase stems, however, from the word "community," community of scholars. The invention of the Middle Ages lies in the establishment of a *communitas,* something shared in common, a community of interest, among scholars. In effect, what these medieval scholars did was to bring individuals who had previously functioned largely in isolation into a group with a special identity; they formed with their members a single body, or, as we would say today, they established a corporation. Indeed, the word "university," *universitas,* was in origin nothing but a synonym for denoting this same process of incorporation. Its very etymology implies *turning* a group of individuals into *one* body. Over time, the use of the word *university* was restricted to one particular kind of corporation, to the community of scholars, to a university as we use the word today.

Most of the actual steps in the development of a university in the twelfth and thirteenth centuries are shrouded in obscurity, and historians argue over the dates at which given institutions may be said to have been established. Understandings among individual scholars in Paris, for example, and the outward recognition of these by others, emerge successively and not all at once. The general direction of development is clear in any case. The progression is in the direction away from the individualistic tutor to what might be called the group practice of scholarly teaching with the adoption of regulations affecting the government of the affairs of the community of scholars, the status of the master scholars or teachers or professors, the status of the student scholars, and the prescription of courses of instruction.

Finally there was the matter of the degree or license. You know that the phrase "community of scholars" is used with a connotation that embraces both the faculty and the students, the old learners, as it were, and the new learners. This was quite appropriate in the medieval setting. The older scholars taught the younger scholars in a particular way. In accordance with the technology of the time and the characteristics of the bookish, learned traditions of that day, the teachers lectured; that is, they read passages from the costly manuscript books that contained the accumulated learning of the past and then brought in more recent or contemporary insights by commenting upon the texts. A lecture was thus a combination of reading out loud and of talking. When the students had imbibed a fair measure of this learning by listening to the prescribed course of lectures and through disputation, that is, discussion largely among themselves, and had cut their own teeth on the substance, they might be ready to try the examinations. They would appear before a board composed of teachers or professors and there be quizzed as to their knowledge and, if approved, be given permission to proceed to the final demonstration of proficiency, namely, to do what the master or professor characteristically did himself as a learned man, that is, to give a lecture on a learned topic. This beginning (*inceptio*) of the practice of the master or teacher is the origin of the commencement address, which in its proper ancient form was delivered by the graduating students.

At the same time, the successful candidate would, by a ceremonial gesture, be admitted to the grade of, the status of, the degree of a bachelor or master. The routine granting of a diploma is a fairly late form. In this country, at Harvard, it was not until 1813 that all graduates received a diploma as a matter of course. Doctor Pusey's predecessor, at the first Harvard commencement in 1642, following the rhetorical performances of the graduating students, their commencing lectures, turned to each and said: "I admit thee to the first degree in Arts . . . according to the custom of the universities in England. And I hand thee this book, together with the powers to lecture publicly in any one of the arts which thou hast studied, whensoever thou shalt have been called to that office." Here, as a proof of admittance to higher learning, there were still linked the book, the text, and the right to lecture upon it. The book was, of course, purely symbolic; and in all honesty I must reveal, Dr. Pusey, that your predecessor appears to have been an Indian giver and to have taken back these books immediately. Harvard men do not seem subsequently to have held this ungenerosity against their alma mater. Indeed, they have returned the gift many fold in their magnificent contributions to the Harvard libraries. There are still, in my judgment, important meanings in this medievalism for our time. Scholars, teachers possessed of the most advanced knowledge of their time, professors as we would say today, had existed before. Such men, by very definition, must be highly individualistic self-starters, impelled by their own curiosity to seek knowledge, great lovers of that elusive mistress, truth. They can be recognized and given opportunities for pursuing their work, appealed to for various causes, but hardly directed in their professional work as scholars. Who could have told Einstein what to do next? But they can be brought together by persuasion to work in a common enterprise in a way that makes the whole greater than the sum of the several parts.

What the Middle Ages established as a beginning was that such men, by grouping themselves together, by establishing the group practice of scholarship through the creation of a university, could enlarge greatly their own capacity for learning and for teaching. Individual scholars have made contributions to human history, but the establishment of the community of scholars has placed the learned and scientific traditions of mankind on a far firmer footing. It has made available systematic education of the younger generation at the higher levels so that each successive generation could build more solidly and more quickly upon the work of its predecessors. Scholars themselves, to deal with the present frontiers of knowledge, now require facilities in libraries and laboratories that can only be provided through a collective enterprise. Through participation in the community of the university, they can advance knowledge far more rapidly than they could individually in isolation.

The powers that be even in the thirteenth century already showed respect for the community of scholars through papal and royal charters and privileges that guaranteed an autonomous life for the emerging universities. The tradition of university autonomy has come down into our own American history, in which it is found that universities usually have been accorded a very special position. Education itself, from highest to lowest levels, was exempted by the founding fathers from federal control. Even at the state level it was protected through self-denying constitutions and statutes of the several states from strong statewide controls. Basic responsibility for elementary and secondary education was delegated largely to local school boards, which in turn have been kept separate from other branches of local government such as the cities and towns. At the level of higher education, universities under private auspices were encouraged and actually patronized under various provisions of the law that granted them privileges and large immunities. And, when the states established universities under public auspices, they were given a substantial measure of autonomy by a variety of expedients, including in some states even constitutional status to limit control from other branches of state government. They have not been regarded as ordinary departments of state government under the control of the executive branch or as subject to conventional policy management by the legislatures.

This tradition of relatively great autonomy for universities in relation to government, stemming from medieval concepts, should not be dismissed as an archaic remain. There are continuing reasons for maintaining it. A degree of vigilance is needed just now in the United States because there has been a movement among some administrators in state government circles in the name of what they construe as efficiency to try to assimilate universities, at least the state universities, into just another branch of state government. Such a view is out of touch with our basic tradition and law, as I have indicated, and, perhaps even more importantly, with the wisdom of the case.

Autonomy for universities is not a matter of special privilege for professors, presidents, or regents. It is a condition for the efficient performance of the tasks of the university. While the university might have been an invention in the first instance of scholars, it quickly came to be seen by others as a kind of insurance policy that society could take out as a guarantee of a better future. It is the special business of universities to encourage a second look at men and matter. They need maneuvering room for their continuing reanalysis of the universe and what is contained therein. They need a large amount of freedom in determining their own program in research and in teaching, for they alone contain the men truly competent to make the necessary judgments. The autonomy granted them is an act of faith by society in the kinds of individuals who pursue the scholarly life of teaching and research, and who are gathered together in a great university. Men in past generations have felt that this act of faith paid off well enough so that through their repeated acts of support universities have been enabled to persist at their task to the point that our oldest corporation still in business in the United States is a university. There are many indications that men still have this confidence today in universities.

I believe you will agree that the need for the contributions of universities to our troubled society is now more evident than ever. This is no time, then, to diminish their capacity to play their peculiar role in society by the misguided imposition of bureaucratic controls from outside persons not equipped to make the highly specialized kinds of judgment required in a university. There is little wisdom—and a great deal of harm—in the application of standards of efficiency that are not appropriate to the functions of universities, however appropriate they may be for other functions.

If one is indeed to espouse the university in these terms, he must face with humility the charge placed upon me today on behalf of the Board of Regents of the University of Washington. The task is large; the responsibility to the university and to society is great. The faculty has already brought distinction to this university and desires to see still greater distinction attained in rendering service. I promise the faculty that I shall try to sense with imagination what is needed in tools for scholarship, in the means of teaching and research, and to find ways by which the faculty may be more adequately, more equitably, supported. I promise no less, as a colleague, to seek to detect ways to improve our own awareness of our common concerns in teaching and research, and to devise channels through which the intellectual energy of the faculty may flow toward the further advancement of knowledge and the improvement of curriculums and teaching.

I promise the younger scholars, the students, that I shall try to find ways that will permit their masters to have that more intimate contact with them on scholarly matters which true teachers always desire so that out of this association there may emerge that love of scholarship which can attend the university-educated man all the days of his life. Even though the graduating student may follow a career different from that of his teaching masters who admitted him to the degree or grade of bachelor or master or doctor, he should have acquired from his professors stimulation for the maintenance of curiosity, encouragement of the habit of study, and the experience of disciplined thinking. The nourishing care of alma mater must stretch the muscles of the student's mind at the risk of an occasional charley horse, but it will be no less loving for all that, and no less in his best interest.

To the alumni who have loved this university, I promise to do what I can do to enlarge still more the basis for their legitimate pride in the institution. I promise also to turn to the alumni increasingly for that extra help in moral and material support that every university needs now from its sons and daughters, its past beneficiaries, if it is to measure up to the mighty task it faces in trying to provide adequate opportunities for the education of their sons and daughters.

To our sister institutions in higher education, so many of whom have graced this occasion with their representatives present here today, I promise to try to be a good neighbor and companion, recognizing our different areas of service and our common ground and need of mutual support.

To His Excellency, the Governor, and the honorable members of the Legislature of the State of Washington, I promise advocacy of the realistic needs of the university as it strives to be nothing less than a great university, serving greatly the people of the state as a human monument fit to match the inspiring mountains and distant perspectives nature has lavished upon us here, a leader among institutions and not a follower, a pioneer among pioneers as great universities must by definition ever strive to be.

I reread recently *The Aims of Education* of Alfred North Whitehead in the paperback edition. It contains a brief but wonderful appreciation of him by Mr. Justice Frankfurter. The mere reading of it caused a warm feeling to flow over me, for I was one of that generation of students privileged to be invited into those wonderful Sunday evening coffee and conversation sessions in the Whiteheads' apartment overlooking the Charles River. The breadth of the man, the depth of insight, that humility coupled with courage—yes, and gentle humor—in facing the awesome mysteries of the universe that surround us and that open up like a chasm within us radiated through his conversation as well as through his lectures. So, too, did his firm belief in man's use of reason, however blunted it might be, before the profound complexities of the world, and his conviction that the universities had to be the guardians and caretakers of this intellectual civilization.

Mr. Frankfurter quotes Professor Whitehead as follows:

> The Aegean Coastline had its chance and made use of it; Italy had its chance and made use of it; France, England, Germany had their chance and made use of it. Today the Eastern American states have their chance. What use will they make of it? That question has two answers. Once Babylon had its chance, and produced the Tower of Babel. The University of Paris fashioned the intellect of the Middle Ages.[1]

The Eastern American states, he says, have their chance. So indeed they do, and they have done well by it. The splendid example, to cite only one, that Harvard presents to the world today, Dr. Pusey, we unhesitatingly and gratefully acknowledge.

Professor Whitehead voyaged far in his own lifetime. He

[1] Alfred North Whitehead, *The Aims of Education* (New York: New American Library, 1949), p. 9.

liked adventures in living as well as in ideas. His historical sense taught him how the torch of learning had passed from Greece to Rome to Paris to modern Germany, and England, and to the Eastern states of the United States. He himself helped in this westward pilgrimage of learning by moving from the old Cambridge in England to the new Cambridge in Massachusetts. If he were alive today, pondering on these matters a quarter century later, he would not have been surprised, I believe, by the thought that the Western states might have their chance too.

But he would have noted a change. The westward movement has now gone virtually full circle to meet the Levant, to flow into the lands of the rising sun; and there sits in our consciousness the realization that we are all now caught up in this global world in a troubled time. More is demanded than that the torch be tended now here, now there, as it is passed along. We are all in this world together, and it is imperative that the torches of learning be held aloft and tended in many places. In purely national terms it is not enough to have a handful of great universities for a country of 175,000,000, and those mostly in the East. If this intellectual civilization that Whitehead prized is to survive and prosper in these United States, there must be a string of creative, I repeat, creative universities from East to West and from North to South. The Western states must do their part in accepting and building nothing but the best.

Let us be grateful, then, for models elsewhere. May it be given to us to recognize the best when we see it wherever we see it, to strive to emulate it here ourselves, and to do our share in fraternal affection in work in which our universities will ultimately succeed or fail together. We need not fear rivalry. We have far more reason to fear the inadequacy of the efforts of all our universities, the young in years in company with the ancient and venerable, in building around our civilization that wall of intelligence and understanding needed to restrain the eroding forces of ignorance and brutishness that could engulf us all. All of us, Eastern and Western, in and out of universities, must work in the hope that the American people will be enabled to escape the curse that now threatens modern man, the awesome great sentence that was noted by Professor Whitehead in the following words:

> In the conditions of modern life the rule is absolute, the race which does not value trained intelligence is doomed. Not all your heroism, not all your social charm, not all your wit, not all your victories on land or at sea, can move back the finger of fate. To-day we maintain ourselves. To-morrow science will have moved forward yet one more step, and there will be no appeal from the judgment which will then be pronounced on the uneducated.[2]

We must in the Western states take up still more the slack and not rely as much as in the past on what the Eastern states have provided if we are to give our sons and daughters their just due and to enable them and us to acquit ourselves of our fair share of responsibility in preventing all America from receding into the accursed land of the uneducated.

There is, then, a monumental task that faces us here in Washington and at the University of Washington. I know full well that I am but one of many who will serve the University of Washington in these coming years. Each of us has his particular niche in a structure, the University, which far transcends us all. All these people dedicate themselves every day to her service that she may better serve mankind. I do

[2] *Ibid.*, p. 26.

not think it a poetic license to say that once again they are accepting this charge with me here today, grateful, as I am grateful, for the opportunity of service, humble before the responsibility but joyous in work that is pleasure, and hopeful that future generations will conclude that our efforts in our day were mostly on the side of making an understatement of Dr. Suzzallo's name for this institution, the University of a Thousand Years.

PROGRAM OF THE INAUGURATION,
NOVEMBER 6 AND 7, 1958

INAUGURAL SESSIONS

Session on EDUCATION AND AMERICAN SOCIETY

Thursday afternoon, November 6, 2:30 o'clock . . Meany Hall

    Presiding: KENNETH C. COLE
        Professor of Political Science, University of
        Washington

        Education for the Scientific and Industrial Age
            CLARK KERR, *President,* University of California

        Education for a Society of Law
            EUGENE V. ROSTOW, *Dean, School of Law,* Yale
            University

        Education and the Problem of Communication
            ERWIN D. CANHAM, *Editor, Christian Science Monitor*

Session on PHYSICAL AND BIOLOGICAL SCIENCES
AND TECHNOLOGY

Thursday evening, November 6, 8 o'clock . . . Meany Hall

    Presiding: HANS NEURATH
        *Professor and Executive Officer of the Department of
        Biochemistry,* University of Washington

        Physical Science—Present and Future
            POLYKARP KUSCH, *Professor of Physics,* Columbia
            University

        Round Trip from Space
            MELVIN CALVIN, *Director, Bio-organic Chemistry
            Group, Radiation Laboratory,* University of California

Session on THE HUMANITIES IN THE
MODERN WORLD

Friday morning, November 7, 9:30 o'clock . . . Meany Hall

    Presiding: ROBERT B. HEILMAN
        *Professor and Executive Officer of the Department of
        English,* University of Washington

The Place of Literature in the Humanities
  ARTHUR S. P. WOODHOUSE, *Head, Department of English,* University of Toronto, Canada

Modern Art and the Humanities
  G. H. FORSYTH, *Chairman, Department of Fine Arts,* University of Michigan

A Task for the Humanities
  GEORGE BOAS, *Professor Emeritus of Philosophy,* Johns Hopkins University

INAUGURAL CEREMONY

Meany Hall Auditorium

Friday afternoon, November 7, 2:30 o'clock

ORDER OF THE INAUGURAL CEREMONY

Announcer: GORDON D. MARCKWORTH, *Dean of Forestry*

PROCESSIONAL, "Entrance of the Mastersingers" . . WAGNER
University Symphony Orchestra and Sinfonietta
Conductor: Stanley Chapple, *Director of the School of Music,*
University of Washington

PRESENTATION OF THE COLORS . . . ROTC CADETS

"STAR-SPANGLED BANNER" . . . FRANCIS SCOTT KEY
Group singing led by Dena Lampropulos

INVOCATION . THE RIGHT REVEREND STEPHEN F. BAYNE, JR.
Bishop of Olympia

FORMAL OPENING OF THE CEREMONIES
HAROLD S. SHEFELMAN
President of the Board of Regents

GREETINGS FROM THE COMMONWEALTH
ALBERT D. ROSELLINI
Governor of the State of Washington

INSTALLATION ADDRESS . . . . NATHAN M. PUSEY
President of Harvard University

"Fanfare for Brass," written especially for this occasion
STANLEY CHAPPLE

"Academic Festival Overture" . . . . BRAHMS
University Symphony Orchestra and Sinfonietta

INDUCTION OF THE PRESIDENT . HAROLD S. SHEFELMAN
President of the Board of Regents

INAUGURAL ADDRESS . . . CHARLES EDWIN ODEGAARD
President of the University

BENEDICTION . THE MOST REVEREND THOMAS A. CONNOLLY
Archbishop of Seattle

RECESSIONAL, "Alla marcia" (Karelia Suite) . . . SIBELIUS
University Symphony Orchestra and Sinfonietta

INAUGURAL BANQUET

Grand Ballroom, Olympic Hotel
(Dress Optional)

Friday evening, November 7, at 7 o'clock

Toastmaster: THE HONORABLE MATTHEW W. HILL
Chief Justice, Supreme Court, State of Washington

ADDRESSES OF GREETING

FOR THE STUDENTS OF THE UNIVERSITY
LEX GAMBLE, *President of the Associated Students*

FOR THE UNIVERSITY ALUMNI
HOWARD TUTTLE, *President of the Alumni Association*

FOR THE UNIVERSITY FACULTY
ROSS A. BEAUMONT, *Chairman of the University Senate*

FOR THE BOARD OF REGENTS
HAROLD S. SHEFELMAN, *President of the Board of Regents*

FOR THE STATE OF WASHINGTON
ALBERT D. ROSELLINI, *Governor of the State of Washington*

FOR THE PRIVATE INSTITUTIONS
ALBERT A. LEMIEUX, S.J., *President of Seattle University*

FOR THE PUBLIC INSTITUTIONS
C. CLEMENT FRENCH, *President of State College of Washington*

RESPONSE

CHARLES EDWIN ODEGAARD
President of the University of Washington

THE BOARD OF REGENTS OF THE UNIVERSITY

HAROLD S. SHEFELMAN, Seattle, *President*
JOHN L. KING, Seattle, *Vice-President*
THOMAS BALMER, Seattle
MRS. A. SCOTT BULLITT, Seattle
JOSEPH DRUMHELLER, Spokane
MRS. J. HERBERT GARDNER, La Conner
CHARLES M. HARRIS, Entiat

COMMITTEES ON THE PRESIDENT'S INAUGURATION

REGENTS' COMMITTEE

HAROLD S. SHEFELMAN, *Chairman,* assisted by the entire Board

FACULTY COMMITTEE

ROY E. LINDBLOM (Engineering), *Chairman*
EDWARD G. BROWN (Business Administration)
BYRON H. CHRISTIAN (Communications)
JOHN E. CORBALLY (Education)
GEORGE W. FARWELL (Physics)
ALFRED HARSCH (Law)
JAMES W. HAVILAND (Medicine)
W. STULL HOLT (History)
VIRGINIA OLCOTT (Nursing)

DIVISIONAL COMMITTEES

Social Sciences

EDWARD G. BROWN (Business Administration), *Chairman*
BYRON H. CHRISTIAN (Communications)
ALFRED HARSCH (Law)

Sciences

GEORGE W. FARWELL (Physics), *Chairman*
JAMES W. HAVILAND (Medicine)
BLAKE D. MILLS (Engineering)
VIRGINIA OLCOTT (Nursing)
HERSCHEL L. ROMAN (Botany)

Humanities

W. STULL HOLT (History), *Chairman*
JOHN E. CORBALLY (Education)